JAGUAR XK FORTY YEARS ON

Andrew Whyte

Aston Publications Limited

Sole distributors for the USA
Motorbooks International
Publishers & Wholesalers Inc.

Published in 1988 by Aston Publications Limited
Bourne End House
Harvest Hill
Bourne End
Bucks SL8 5JJ

British Library Cataloguing in Publication Data

Whyte, Andrew
1. Motor vehicles. Jaguar XK engines to 1988.
I. Title
629. 2′ 504

ISBN 0-946627- 41 - X

Designed by Chris Hand

Printed in Hong Kong

Sole distributors to the U.K. book trade,
Springfield Books Ltd.
Norman Road, Denby Dale
Huddersfield
West Yorkshire HD8 8TH

Sole distributors for the USA
Motorbooks International
Osceola, Wisconsin 54020
United States

Early batch of XK engines at Swallow Road, Coventry, 1949.

7
OKV 2

Introduction

The superlatives began in October 1948, when Earls Court opened its doors for London's first motor show in ten years.

Times were still hard, but after three years of an austere peacetime the world and his wife were ready for some excitement. Fuel rationing and high export quotas meant that the buyer's market remained a dream, even for the wealthy or specially privileged; but now that dream could be turned into temporary reality as bright colours gleamed once more in the Aladdin's Cave of SW5.

The 'big six' were there, of course. Austin and the Nuffield Group (still several years away from their merger) were vying for variety, the latter creating a great sensation with its Morris Minor. Ford had plenty up its sleeve, but, meantime, was clinging to pre-war concepts. By contrast Rootes, Standard and GM (Vauxhall) now effected the 'new look'. It was the first appearance for the Land-Rover all-purpose vehicle–shown in estate-car form –whereas Rover's four and six light saloons retained their traditional and restrained good looks. It was a show of infinite variety, old and new ideas blending or conflicting. The way ahead was still uncertain. Some companies had been kept alive on war contracts, but had not planned ahead. Dressing up old bones was to prove fatal for many famous names in the ensuing years. As world trade recovered, they did not.

On the other hand, those with foresight and ambition were investing for the inevitable industrial explosion. One such company was Jaguar (formerly SS Cars Ltd), which had just introduced its Mark V–a distinguished-looking car with a new chassis featuring wishbone and torsion-bar independent front suspension, but retaining the general appearance and mechanical layout of its predecessor. For William Lyons and his team, who had worked up on many discarded mock-ups before choosing this design, it was known that the Mark V was an interim model; yet it would give the marque a strong image as markets began to open up. Few people outside the company knew that a completely new engine was being tested in one of the cars.

The Mark V's regular power unit was a straight-six of 2.7 and 3.5 litres displacement, built by Jaguar on equipment mainly acquired from the Standard company, originators of the engine that Harry Weslake had been authorized to develop as an overhead valve conversion exclusively for Lyons, back in the 1930s.

For several years, however, a twin overhead camshaft engine of all-Jaguar design had been under development. Indeed, not long before the 1948 show, a high-compression four-cylinder version of it was known to have propelled Col. Gardner's streamlined 'special' along a Belgian motorway at over 175 mph. Nevertheless, it came as a genuine last-minute sensation to Press and public alike when those Earls Court covers were pulled back to reveal—alongside the Mark V—a completely new open Jaguar two-seater with a six-cylinder 'twin-cam' engine. On 27 October 1948 *The Motor* summed up the element of surprise that followed a speech by William Lyons when introducing the Mark V in late September. He had 'made a direct reference to the intention to produce a sports car', but 'what was not generally anticipated was that the new sports model would be at the Motor Show' so soon afterwards. The fact that the car—the 'XK120'—and its engine were by no means ready for production simply emphasized Lyon's opportunism and confidence in the future. 'XK' came from the engine's designation, '120' from the car's anticipated maximum speed in miles per hour. If looks alone counted, the '120' figures had to be conservative and events would prove them to be so.

In pre-war days, the SS Jaguar '100' sports car had been built in small quantities—only a few more than three hundred in a four-year period. At a production rate averaging around six a month, it had provided prestige for the marque without interfering with the main assembly area of the factory. It is probable that Lyons visualized a similar arrangement for the new '120', but the response to his bronze bombshell at Earls Court in 1948 made him change his mind. The first 240 Jaguar XK120s were built in the traditional manner with aluminium panels over wood and steel. In early 1950, however, when full-scale production got under way, a change was made to more modern pressed steel construction (over 12,000 XK120s had been made by late 1954 when the XK140 came along). In late 1950, the Mark V was supplemented—later to be replaced—by the Mark VII, the modern Jaguar saloon for which the Mark V's chassis and the XK120's engine had been proposed from the project's outset.

For the next two decades, every single new Jaguar car was produced with an XK engine, which would remain the staple power unit after the V-12 was introduced in 1971 and right through to the 1987 model year when the long-awaited 'XJ40' became the second-generation XJ6. Even then, the 'XK' would still be specified for the Daimler limousine and for military applications.

Forty years after its announcement, the Jaguar XK engine was still being produced in limited quantities, and looked like remaining so into the 1990s. Its longevity and popularity among automotive specialists of all kinds will ensure that the Jaguar XK engine is considered as an all-time classic when, in due course, enthusiasts and engineers look back at it from the twenty-first century.

This book is not intended as a discourse on the design, construction, development or rebuilding of the XK engines. All these matters have been handled in many ways by many authors on many occasions; and some suggested in-depth reading is included with the tabular material at the back of this book.

The XK engine may possess no single astounding features; but in the combination of its virtues it stands above all other double-ohc units.

Designed for performance and long life, the XK gave a nominal 160 bhp when it was introduced—and it went on to meet its creators' requirements of major development potential with well over double that amount being shown in competition units later on. It is an engine which proved it could win the 24-hour race at Le Mans five times or propel a car at over 100 mph average for a whole week. It could produce the best performance in tough road events like the Alpine and Monte Carlo rallies and the notorious *Marathon de la Route.* Yet it could operate quietly—*not* a traditional feature of twin chain-driven camshafts—and flexibly in everyday use. Moreover the Jaguar engine's looks matched its capabilities – another Lyons requirement – and to view the engine compartment of an XK-powered car was to witness automotive artistry, as applies in the case of any restored or well-maintained vehicle today.

Other makers, such as Lagonda (whose W. O. Bentley-designed engine would be adapted for the DB2 Aston Martin and its successors), did offer double-ohc 'sixes' at this time – but they were the costly offerings of low-volume producers and did not compare on performance or price. At £988 (or £1263 3*s*. 11*d*. with purchase tax) the XK120 set the parameters for the Jaguar post-war value-for-money reputation. Space was added to Grace and Pace with the Mark VII in October 1950 at just £10 more; £998 plus £277 19*s*. 6*d*. making a total of £1275 19*s*. 6*d*. The UK pricing was fairly academic, since so many cars were sold for overseas currency – particularly in the USA, where Lyons had gone to prepare the market in early 1948.

There have been various engine specifications for the six-cylinder XK engine – and various displacements, the most familiar being 2483, 2792, 3442, 3781 and 4325 cubic centimetres. Originally, it was due to have an 83 x 98 mm (3182 cc) swept volume, but for its public introduction the stroke was increased to 106 mm, which was not altered. The main models and engines are listed at the end of this book.

Before telling the XK story in pictures (which is what I have set out to do) I should like to thank Jaguar Cars Ltd, Alvis Ltd, Graham Gauld, Guy Griffiths, Paul Skilleter and the many others who have helped make it tellable. On behalf of all those lucky enough to own or use XK-engined vehicles, I must acknowledge not only the late Sir William Lyons, Harry Weslake and Claude Baily, but above all Bill Heynes and Walter Hassan. This book is a small tribute to them for providing so much practical service and pleasure to so many people on road and race circuits around the world – and to Trevor Crisp for his part in developing the XK for the age of emission controls, without which Jaguar's strong presence in North America would not have continued. In fact, it would be true to say that without the XK engine's great adaptability and character, the very survival of Jaguar today could not have occurred – and the XK engine is far from dead. Long live the XK engine.

ANDREW WHYTE

Sir William Lyons, Jaguar's founder and chief executive, with Her Majesty Queen Elizabeth and a D-type. (Jaguar XK-engined cars won the 24-hour Le Mans *Grand Prix d'Endurance* five times.) Also in this 1956 Browns Lane Works picture is H.R.H. Prince Philip, talking to William Heynes and John Silver (Production Director).

Sir William Lyons with Johannes Eerdmans (head of Jaguar Cars Inc) at the 1962 New York show for the US debut of the Mark Ten, clearly identifiable by the gleam of its triple SU carburettors.

The men behind the Jaguar XK engine: technical director William Heynes (*left*), chief development engineer Walter Hassan (*below left*), and designer Claude Baily (*below right*).

Many different experimental engine designs were examined before the 'XK' was settled upon. This 1945 'XG' (*right*) was one of the more significant ones. It would have had a single camshaft in the cylinder block, operating cross-over pushrods in the BMW manner. It was based on the existing 4-cylinder Standard (1776 cc) cylinder block, and its inclined ohv layout gave it the good looks upon which William Lyons insisted. It might have been cheap to make, too, but it was rejected in favour of the all-new XK engine–perhaps because its downdraught induction might have called for a raised body line?

The XK engine was intended as a 4- and 6-cylinder 'family', and both types were well on the way to volume production when the 'four', seen here (*above right*), was shelved. With a claimed power output of 105 bhp at 5000 rpm, and bore and stroke of 80.5 mm and 98 mm respectively, it had been proposed as the motive power for an XK100 sports car. Its only 'public' appearance, however, was as a record-breaker in Col. A. T. G. Gardner's aerodynamic car, formerly the MG known as EX135.

Right: Race-tuned to produce 146 bhp, the 4-cylinder Jaguar engine is enveloped by the streamlined body of the Gardner Special, which took international 2-litre class records at nearly 177 mph in this form on the Belgian autoroute in 1948.

Left: The 1955 cc 4-cylinder engine, as installed in the Gardner Special.

Top left: Cross-section of 6-cylinder XK engine as released for production in 1949: a 3442 cc long-stroke unit (83 mm x 106 mm) with seven-bearing crankshaft.

The longitudinal section (*below*) and the cross-section (*right*) show the arrangement of the camshaft chain drive and sprocket assembly chosen to minimize noise.

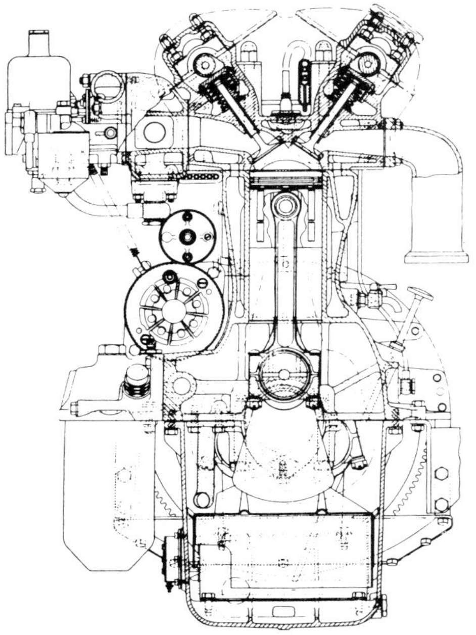

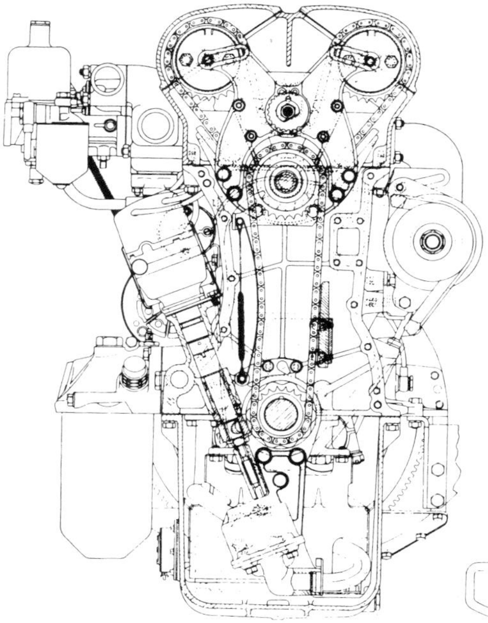

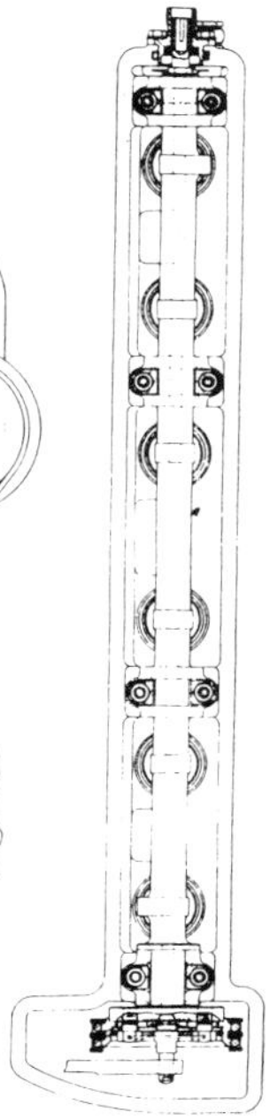

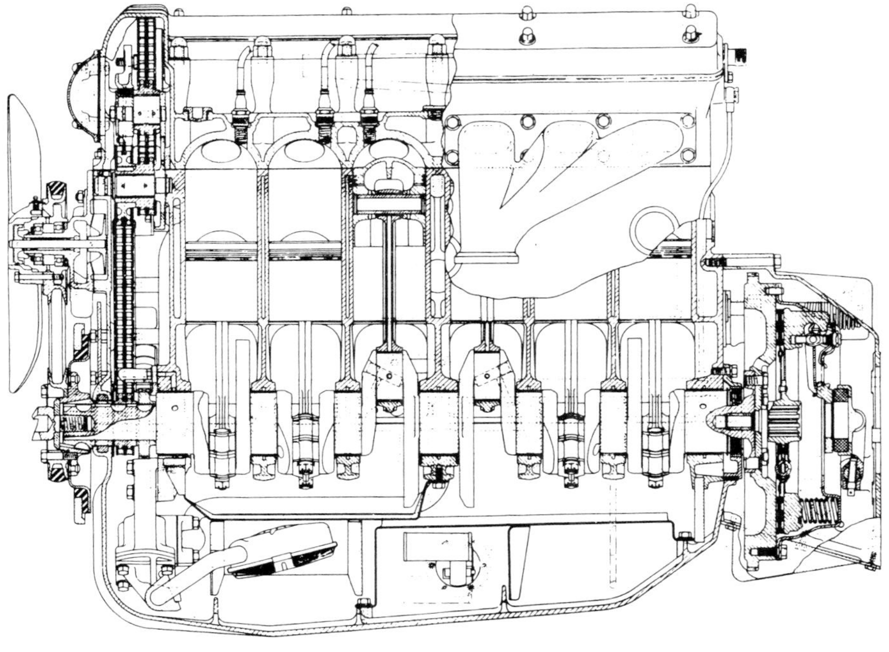

XK 6-cylinder 3.4-litre double overhead camshaft engine, as illustrated in the leaflet, ADVANCE PARTICULARS OF THE NEW JAGUAR TYPE XK 100 and 120 SUPER SPORTS MODELS, published in February 1949.

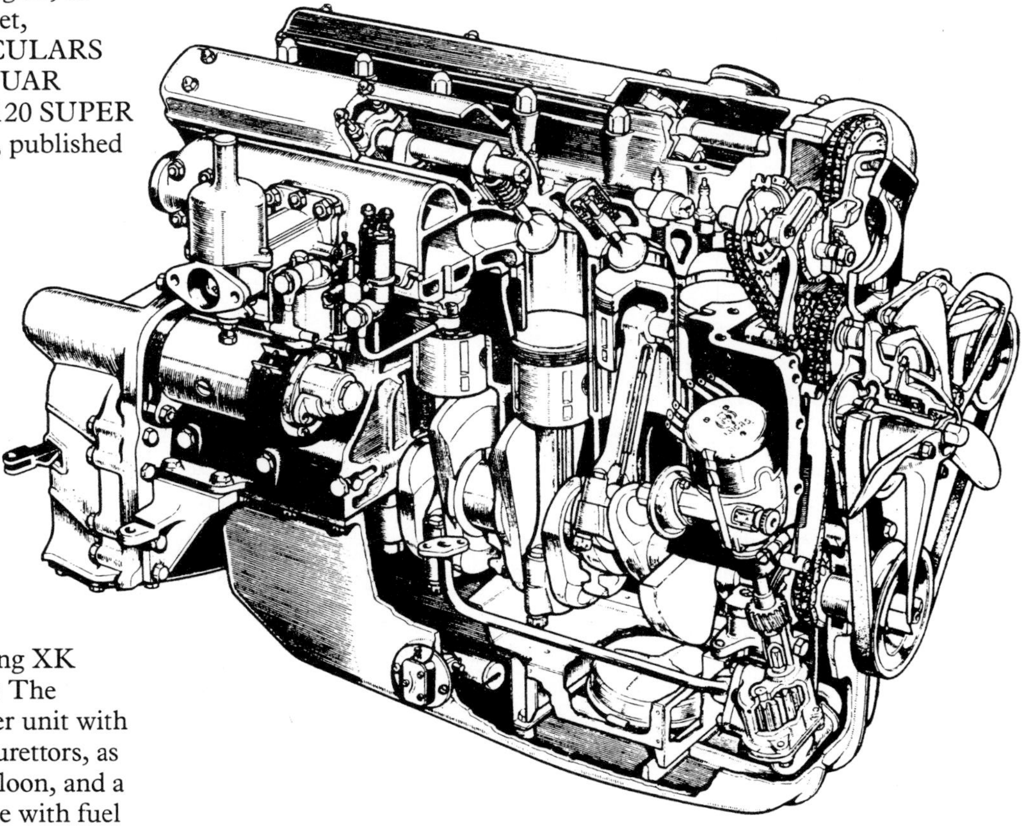

Below: Two contrasting XK engines of the 1960s: The regular 4.2-litre power unit with twin 2-inch SU carburettors, as fitted into the XJ6 saloon, and a 3.8-litre racing engine with fuel injection.

Early production XK engines on the test-bed, probably photographed shortly before the move from Swallow Road to the Browns Lane Works, Coventry, 1951, before the days of automatic transmission. The shorter gear lever was for the XK120 model, the straight one for the Mark Seven saloon.

Experimental department tester R. M. V. Sutton in Swallow Road with XK120 prepared for high-speed demonstration runs, which took place in Belgium in May 1949. The car averaged 132.596 mph for the flying mile, and hit the headlines as a result.

Despite a mild contretemps, Leslie Johnson won the very first major post-war production car race in August 1949, during the International *Daily Express* Silverstone meeting. Another XK120 driven by Peter Walker was second in this one-hour event. HKV 500 was converted to have a right-hand driving position for this purpose. This famous car's subsequent achievements included outright victory in the 1951 Liège-Rome-Liège high-speed rally, with Jöhnny Claes at the wheel.

HKV 500's engine, as installed for Silverstone, 1949.

In early 1950, six XK120s (Chassis Nos. 660040-44 and 660057) were competition-prepared at the Swallow Road, Coventry, works of Jaguar Cars Ltd. The first of these to compete anywhere was 660043 (*above*), registered JWK 650, which went to Italy for the use of Italy's road-race King, Clemente Biondetti. In this picture he is seen with Jaguar's race engineer John Lea and his own mechanic, Giancarlo Bronzoni, arriving at Palermo for Targa Florio scrutineering in spring 1950. Biondetti ran second to Ascari (Ferrari) for nearly half the race, then No. 3 connecting rod broke and holed the engine. Lea sent back the sketch (*inset*) for Bill Heynes with a note making it clear that the engine had not been over-revved, but that there were 'definite indications' that a forging crack had initiated this failure across the stiffening web and through the bearing housing. As a direct result of this experience, Jaguar would introduce the crack-testing of all XK engine connecting rods. Truly, racing began improving the breed from the very start: and there *was* some solace for Jaguar, and Biondetti, for the retirement of all the competitive Ferraris was put down to the pressure to which they had been subjected by the XK120, while the race went to Alfa Romeo.

Shortly afterwards, with a new engine from the works, Biondetti did well in the Mille Miglia, coming eighth despite having to get a broken spring clamped by a blacksmith. He was second fastest from Rome back to Brescia, and expressed the belief that the car had the pace to win. In May he came third in the Parma-Poggio di Berceto race, then bent the chassis in a crash during the Giro dell' Umbria.

While repairs to the car went ahead slowly, Biondetti had the rebuilt Targa Florio engine fitted into a 'special' of his own. This was entered as a Jaguar-Ferrari in the Italian Grand Prix at Monza, completing fifteen laps before retiring. This was the only World Championship Formula One event ever in which a Jaguar engine took part. The Biondetti Special with the works Jaguar engine did, however, achieve some subsequent success as a sports car, and was re-bodied for 1952 (see page 42).

Alfonso Gomez Mena gives the Jaguar XK120 roadster its first overseas race victory, in a Cuban national production car event on 24 February 1950. He is also at the wheel in the picture below with Frank Seiglie, Jaguar's newly-appointed Havana agent, who prepared the car. (The XK120's first race abroad had taken place in the previous month at Palm Beach Shores, Florida, where Leslie Johnson had come fourth overall and won the Production Car trophy.)

Sir William Lyons (1901-1985), the man who created the Jaguar marque, from its value and style to the determination of its advanced technical specifications. He is seen (*above left*) in his retirement year of 1972, when he was seventy. The other two pictures were taken at his home (Wappenbury, near Leamington Spa) in the early 1980s, with Lady Greta Lyons and the man who had joined Jaguar to rebuild it in the post-BL era–John Egan.

Beginning with the XK120's successful racing debut there in 1949 with the famous HKV 500 driven by Leslie Johnson, Silverstone was the scene of XK-powered Jaguar international race victories annually for fifteen years–first with sports cars, then saloons, and finally grand touring cars.

Below: Whilst the Jaguar Mk 5 Drophead coupé and saloon models were the Company's last vehicles to be fitted with the pre-war design of ohv engine, this picture shows the experimental car of William Lyons, registered JBC 441, which had the XK120 engine installed. This photograph was taken shortly before the move to Browns Lane in 1951.

In September 1950, on the eve of his twenty-first birthday, Stirling Moss gave himself and Jaguar their first long-distance race win, in the Tourist Trophy, held on the Dundrod road circuit near Belfast in miserable conditions (see page 27). It was to be another year or so before wire wheels and other sporting options became available for the XK120. That 1950 TT winner, JWK 988, was originally owned by Tommy Wisdom, who had driven it in other events, including the Mille Miglia. Brought back to life in the 1980s, this famous car is seen below. In the lower photograph it is being driven by its restorer, David Cottingham, in a Mille Miglia 'retrospective' event.

Probably the best known of all alloy-bodied XK120s is the unrestored NUB 120 (Chassis No. 660044), seen re-united in the 1980s with Sir William Lyons' daughter Patricia, who, as Mrs Appleyard, competed regularly with it between 1950 and 1953. Of all NUB 120's achievements, none surpasses the Appleyards' Alpine Gold Cup – the first of only a few ever awarded, for three successive *Coupes des Alpes*. The Roy Nockolds painting (*right*) shows the car *en route* to its third *Coupe* in 1952. It was exchanged for a similar car in mid-1953 and has remained in active retirement ever since. Below is Ian Stewart with his Ecurie Ecosse XK120 at Silverstone in 1952, photographed by T. C. March.

414
NUB 120
414
ALPES

Announced in late 1950, the Jaguar Mark Seven was the first all-new post-war Jaguar saloon; indeed it was the car for which the XK engine was primarily intended, although its power unit had become well known in the two years since the XK120 roadster's introduction. Despite being large and heavy, its power and its torsion bar suspension made it surprisingly nimble, and it won the first five of Silverstone's celebrated entertainments for touring cars. Here is Stirling Moss, out on his own in the very first Silverstone touring car race, in 1952. (*T. C. March*)

The Mark Seven in its original form had a beautiful and feline grace which has made the Jaguar saloon car distinguishable from all others. It was followed by the more ornate 1957-model Mark Eight (*below*) and, in late 1958, by the Mark Nine, which looked identical but had the bonuses of power-assisted steering, disc brakes all round, and the first production application of the 87 mm bore (3781 cc) version of the XK engine, featuring twin SU HD6 carburettors; this took the nominal gross output up from 190 bhp to 220 bhp at 5500 rpm.

The Mark Seven's last victory at Silverstone was in May 1956 when Ivor Bueb was the winner with this car, registered OVC 69, leading to the line Austin A90 Westminster of Ken Wharton.

(*Below:*) The Mark Seven's moment of greatest glory came in January 1956. It had been runner-up and team-prize winner before, but this time it won the most famous rally of them all – the Monte Carlo – outright. Crewed by Ronald Adams (*right*), Derek Johnston, and Frank Bigger (*left*) this car finished ahead of the Mercedes-Benz of Walter Schock, the Sunbeam of Peter Harper and the rest of a large entry list.

General layout of the Jaguar XK120 chassis with torsion bar and wishbone independent front suspension, and Burman recirculating-ball steering.

Below: Artwork for the Jaguar XK120 catalogue.

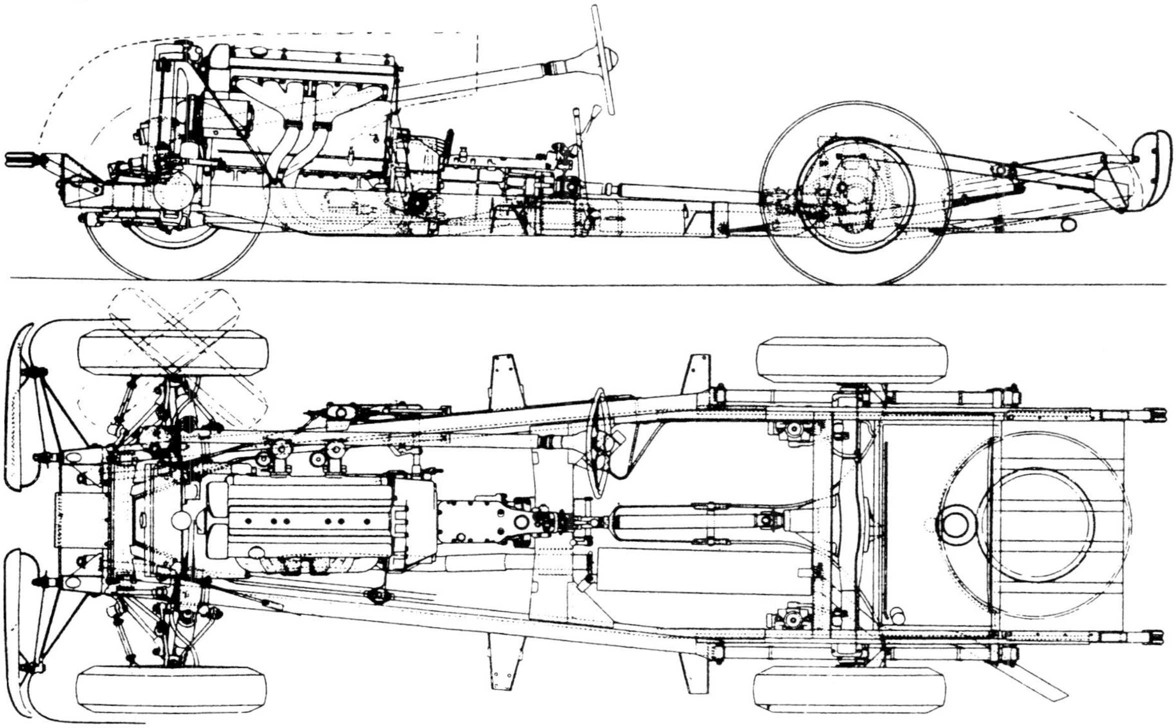

Works Jaguar engine in Biondetti GP Special at Monza in 1950 (*above left*) and later (*above right*) in the same car with mudguards and lamps fitted. Clemente Biondetti is seen (*below*) breaking the course record for his home event, the Firenze-Fiesole hill-climb, in April 1951. A Ferrari 166 body hides the Biondetti-fabricated frame and the works Jaguar engine.

Three of the works-prepared XK120s took part at Le Mans in 1950 (*above*) and proved that, with less brake fade (and less weight), Jaguar had a 24-hour race-winner in the making. One got as high as second, but broke its clutch and retired. Taking things easier, the other two finished twelfth and fifteenth.

Below: Stirling Moss wins the 1950 Tourist Trophy race at Dundrod, N. Ireland, in appalling conditions, driving the sixth of the 1950 works-prepared cars, No. 660057. This car was restored in the 1980s (*see page 19*).

From 1951, the alternative of a fixed-head coupé body was available for the XK120 chassis. This was the year of the works' move from Swallow Road to Browns Lane, where this picture was taken.

Although obsolescent as a competition car, the XK140 enabled Ian Appleyard to take second place to Lyndon Sims (Aston Martin) in the 1956 RAC Rally.

The last phase of the XK series was the XK150 range, which had disc brakes all round, as can be seen in this picture. It was introduced in drophead and fixed-head coupé forms in 1957, but the more attractive roadster was not added until 1958 (see page 65), when the triple-carburettor 'gold top' engine (still 3.4 litres) became an alternative. The XK150 range was complicated further in its final years–1959 and 1960–by the option of twin *and* triple carburettor versions of the new 3.8-litre engine. There was now a choice of four XK power outputs, rated at 210 and 220 bhp for the regular 3.4 and 3.8 engines, and 250/265 for the equivalent straight-port units. Cars with the more powerful ('gold top') engines were named 'XK150S'.

While the XK120/140/150 became more of a 'GT' range as it got old, the XK engine continued to be developed for endurance racing. The chief aim was to dominate the 24-hour Le Mans race and reap the benefits of consequent publicity. The XK120C was produced in time for Le Mans in 1951, featuring a light and rigid steel-tube frame (*above*) quite different from the regular XK120 chassis. This 1951 Le Mans XK engine with high-lift camshafts and other developments by consultant Harry Weslake produced 205 bhp on test, and is seen (*below*) as installed in the brand new XK120C with which Stirling Moss broke the lap record for the Sarthe circuit.

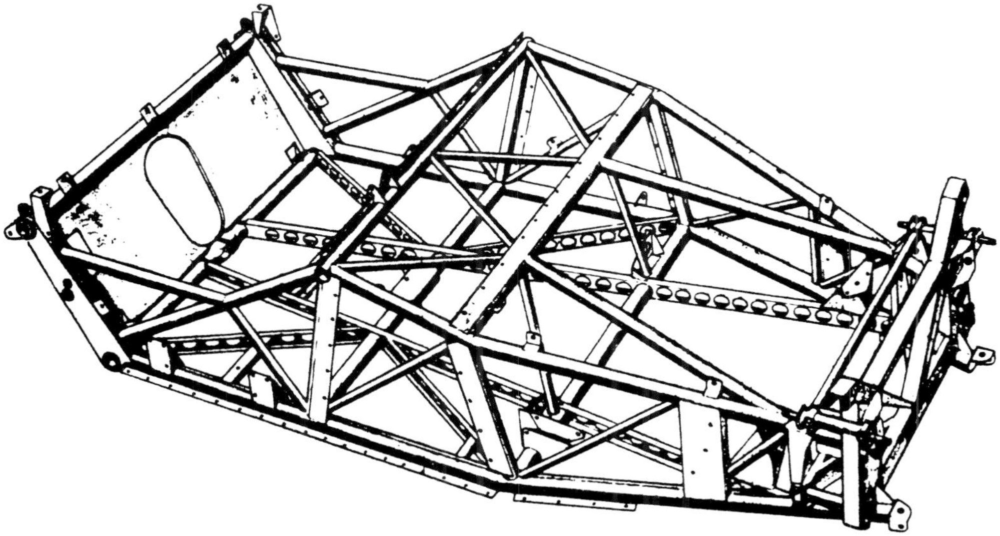

One of the original C-types undergoing preparation for the 1951 Le Mans race. The bonnet retaining straps were later moved to the top of the bonnet.

Below: Peter Whitehead at the wheel of XKC 003 at Le Mans in 1951. On the model's debut he and Peter Walker won the 24 Hours race at a record 93.50 mph. Note the nose, badly scarred by stones.

In the Sports Car race at the International Trophy meeting at Silverstone in May 1952 Peter Walker (XKC 011) leads Tony Rolt (XKC 001). Rolt retired because of failure of the offside rear hub and Walker was classified seventh after a pit stop because of brake problems. Moss won the race with XKC 002.

Below: Stirling Moss at the wheel of his C-type in the opening laps of the 1952 Le Mans race. Fitted with more streamlined noses and tails, the C-types were plagued by overheating. Moss held second place at the end of the first hour, but was forced to retire because a small piece of the timing chain tensioner spring snapped off, worked its way up the oil suction pipe and became stuck under the relief valve.

Production versions of the C-type Jaguar reached the USA in autumn 1952. The first two (*above*) bore the chassis numbers XKC 007 and XKC 009, the latter being in the foreground with George Weaver at the wheel and Jaguar's resident service engineer, R. Graham Reid, wielding the plug-spanner at Elkhart Lake, Wisconsin. This was their debut meeting and Weaver finished third in the Sheldon Cup race, which was won by Phil Hill (in the darker C-type) ahead of Phil Walters in a Ferrari. The close-up (*left*) shows the characteristic twin 2-inch flat-topped SU carburettors of the regular C-type.

Mille Miglia 1953, with from left to right, XKC 008 (Leslie Johnson's car fitted with overdrive), XKC 005 (Tommy Wisdom's car to be driven by Tony Rolt) and XKC 011 (works car for Stirling Moss to be partnered by 'Mort' Morris-Goodall). Tony Rolt (in dark glasses) is to the left of the picture, with Moss and Morris-Goodall to the right. All three cars retired.

Below: Bill Holt with his private C-type, XKC 021 in the Sports Car race at the Grand Prix meeting at Silverstone in July 1953. Following is a privately entered Aston Martin DB3.

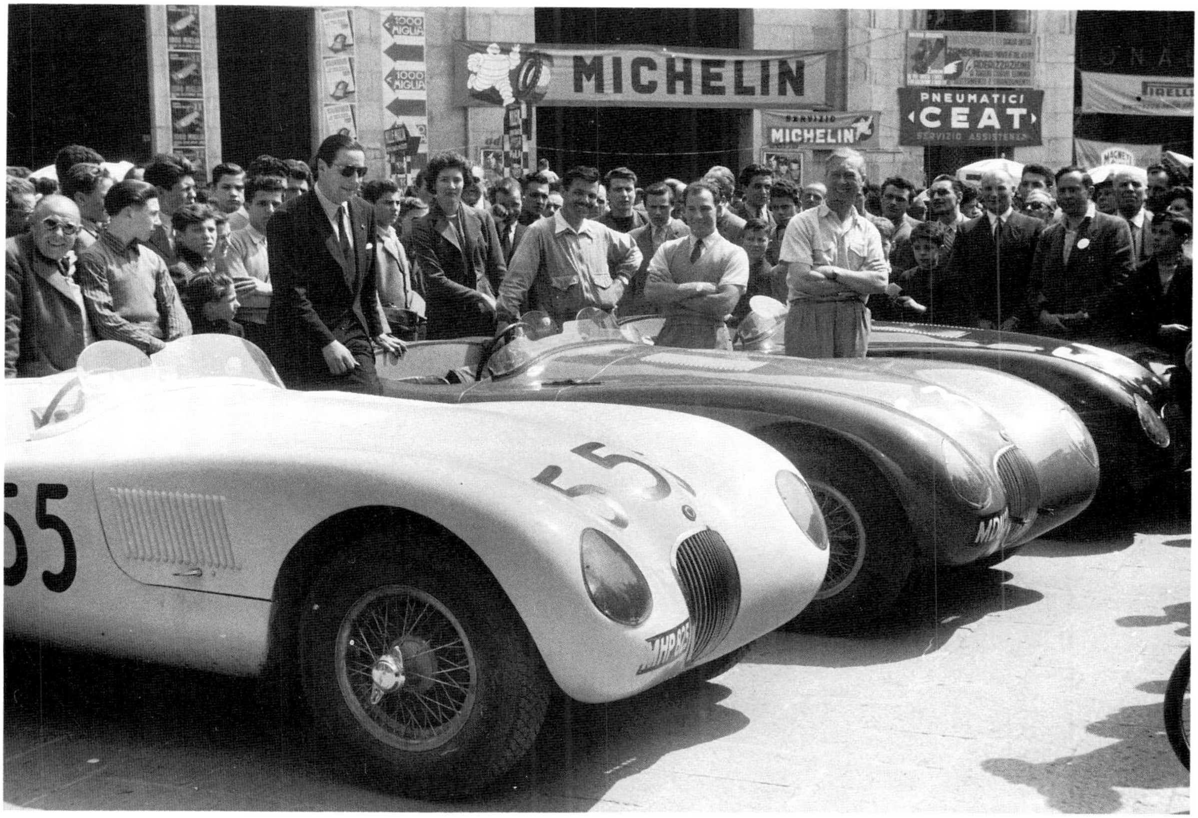

For 1953 Le Mans, the works C-types shed nearly 100 lb in weight. They were fitted with Dunlop disc brakes and triple Weber carburettors, which helped take the bench-tested output up to about 220 bhp. The cars came first, second and fourth in the 24-hour race and afterwards Tony Rolt (*right*) and Duncan Hamilton joined William Lyons (*left*) at Goodwood to show H.R.H. Prince Philip their winning car.

(*Below:*) The 1953 Le Mans-winning C-type joined *Ecurie Ecosse* for 1954, then went to the brilliant Bill Smith in 1955, Geoffrey Allison in 1956 and Miles Brubacher, who spent ten years or so bringing it to the standard shown here (in California, in 1967). The bodywork was still not restored when Brubacher sold it to Briggs Cunningham in 1968. The lightweight body was never refitted, and a new one was made in the 1980s after Duncan Hamilton's son, Adrian, brought the car back to Britain.

Nose shots of two famous competition Jaguars. On the left, D-type XKC 406 (the car that won at Sebring in 1955) and on the right, XKC 038, the C-type built for the 1953 Mexican road race, but not sent. Both cars were photographed at Silverstone in 1967.

Below: Leeds Jaguar distributor Bill Holt with his newly delivered XKC 021, painted suede green, on its debut at the Goodwood meeting in September 1952. (*Guy Griffiths*)

Not a C-type, but the works XK-engined Biondetti Jaguar Special (see page 26) as re-bodied for the 1952 Mille Miglia and other events. It is seen here in the 1984 Mille Miglia 'retrospective' driven by its restorer, Paolo Dabbeni.

Ecurie Ecosse, a private Edinburgh-based team, ran Jaguars from 1952, scoring numerous victories with their smart metallic-blue cars. These C-types (*below*) at Silverstone in 1953 are being driven by the unrelated Ian and Jimmy Stewart. Team boss David Murray's records had Ian driving JWS 353 as usual on this occasion; but the picture clearly indicates that he was in KSF 181. Or could Murray have switched the numbers for some reason?–maybe to confuse history? (He did so on more than one occasion.)

The C-type was the first true competition car from the company, and started the mystique of Jaguar and Le Mans which gave the marque a special cachet. This stood Jaguar in good stead for its survival of the seventies (under BL) to emerge independent in the eighties, when there would be a return to racing with Tom Walkinshaw as the official constructor and team operator. This 1986 picture shows the highly successful Tony Southgate-designed TWR-built 'XJR' sports-prototype at Silverstone, alongside a 35-year-old ex-works Jaguar-designed (*and* built) XK-engined C-type–two brilliant competition cars, purpose-built for their respective eras.

At Silverstone in May 1952 Stirling Moss won the Sports Car race with XKC 002. (*T. C. March*)

Below: Like the C-type, the D-type of 1954, could be used as a road car thanks to the docility of its XK engine which was now developing some 250 bhp on triple Weber carburetters. Here is one of the original works cars, after it had been sold to Jack Broadhead. Usually OKV 2 was driven by Bob Berry, and the small team was managed by Tom Rowe—no mean race *and* rally performer in his own ex-works Mark Seven saloon, here hauling the caravan on a bleak British day.

Tony Rolt with XKC 403 in the Sports Car race at the International Trophy meeting in May 1955. He finished third behind two works Aston Martins. After this race the car was transferred to Jack Broadhead.

Briggs Cunningham did much for Jaguar's reputation, especially between 1955 and 1963–the period in which he ran XK-engined D-types, Listers and E-types. He kept his first D-type–a 1955 long-nose car, XKD 507–in Costa Mesa, California, until he sold his famous collection in 1987. Here he is with the car in 1985. On the left of this picture is glimpsed a unique car, the US-built Cunningham C6R, which began life with an Offenhauser engine but finished up with the impressive Jaguar XK installation seen in the lower picture.

From 1956, Le Mans regulations demanded a full-width windscreen, as fitted to this ex-works long-nose car being driven for *Ecurie Ecosse* by Innes Ireland at Silverstone. The Scottish team's greatest successes by far were its victories at Le Mans in 1956 and 1957. The underbonnet and action shots on this page were taken by Graham Gauld, who played a part in the revival of *Ecurie Ecosse* in the 1980s.

Stirling Moss is en route to victory at Silverstone in 1958, in this fine Graham Gauld shot of the most successful of all the XK-engined hybrids—the Cambridge-built Lister-Jaguar.

Below: Originally raced by Colonel Michael Head and painted white this MKII Cooper-Jaguar is seen in the paddock at Silverstone in 1967.

This Jaguar 'XK120C Series 2' was first seen in mid-1953. That autumn it was fitted with a cockpit cover and under ideal atmospheric conditions touched 180 mph at the Belgian motorway. It was used for test work in early 1954, and is seen being driven by Peter Whitehead (*above*) at Reims. At one stage the car was fitted with fuel injection by SU–but the car and the system were shelved. Instead, in May 1954, the 'XK120C Series 4' was introduced . . . as the D-type (*below*).

The Jaguar D-type was, like the C-type before it, designed to win Le Mans. In fact it was to win three times–but not right away. In 1954 this car (*above*) finished a close second. One of the features of this thoroughly integrated design was the dry-sump lubrication, the oil tank being visible in the foreground. In this pre-race shot, the master himself takes a close interest. Three weeks later, however, Peter Whitehead (*below*) and Ken Wharton drove a sister car to victory in the Reims 12-hour race.

Above: Bearing signs of impatience, XKD 507 brings victory to Sherwood Johnston in the 1955 Watkins Glen Grand Prix. Second and third were Bill Spear (who had partnered Walters in the Jaguar at Le Mans) and Bill Lloyd in 300S Maseratis, ahead of Rich Lyeth and Duncan Black in Ferraris. The group picture (*left*) illustrates the 1957 Cunningham Jaguar team line-up of three D-types and–farthest from camera–the Jaguar-powered Cunningham (see page 46).

Lou Brero at the wheel of XKD 509, painted in distinctive wasp stripes and with battered front end in the 1956 Sebring 12 Hours race. The car ran eighth before retiring.

Below: This long-nose D-type, one of four Jaguar works/Cunningham team cars entered at Sebring in 1956, was driven by Benett/Cunningham, but was delayed by minor problems and eventually finished 12th.

In the Sports Car race at the British Grand Prix meeting at Aintree in July 1955 this D-type, XKD 506, was driven by Mike Hawthorn, but the car was out of its element, it proved no match for the works Aston Martins and Hawthorn had to settle for fifth place.

Below: Ron Flockhart at the wheel of XKD 501 at the start of the 1957 Mille Miglia. It was a most unsuitable car for the race, it suffered from a tendency to shake itself apart on the rough Italian roads and retired because of a loose fuel tank.

A number of specialist constructors built Sports-Racing cars around the XK engine, including above Peter Whitehead's Cooper-Jaguar, the first to be built, at Silverstone in May 1954. The car was fitted with an engine to C-type specification supplied by Jaguar and D-type wheels. This photograph emphasises the extreme off-set driving position, a layout inspired by Piero Taruffi's record-breaking, twin-boom Tarf.

Below: Head-on aspect of Whitehead's Cooper shows distinctly the under-nose shark's mouth radiator air intake, which was soon abandoned, and the detachable covers where head lamps could be fitted.

Over a period of five years H.W.M. successfully raced a whole series of Jaguar powered Sports-Racing cars. This is the first car built in 1953, seen with George Abecassis at the wheel at Goodwood in September 1954.

Below: Seen here in the Sports Car race at the British Grand Prix meeting at Silverstone in 1956 is the later H.W.M.-Jaguar, with at the wheel Noel Cunningham-Reid.
To the right of the photograph is the ex-works Aston Martin DB3S/2 of Tom Kyffin.

The sports-racing cars built around the XK engine by Lister of Cambridge proved superb sprint-race cars, and the Cunningham team raced them in 1958 and 1959. Here Brian Lister and the great driver Archie Scott-Brown discuss the original 1957 car.

Below: Stirling Moss with the works Lister-Jaguar that he drove to a fine win in the Sports Car race at the British Grand Prix meeting at Silverstone in 1958. Between practice and the race, a green surround had been painted round the radiator intake and an engine-bay cooling split opened in the nose. Moss led the race from start to finish.

Jaguar supplied a small quantity of XK engines to Allard. This Palm Beach MkII GT was one of two of the type built and was exhibited at the 1957 London Motor Show.

Below: Here is the Tojeiro-Jaguar seen at Silverstone in July 1958, when Ivor Bueb drove it to fourth place for *Ecurie Ecosse.* Such cars extended the XK engine's competitive life in this field, once Jaguar had disbande its own sports-racing team.

This aluminium prototype, numbered 'E1A', was first driven on the road by Bill Heynes (25 miles) and Sir William Lyons (9 miles) on 17 May 1957. It had a short-stroke 2.4-litre XK engine at that stage. Later it acquired an experimental 3-litre alloy-block engine and Mike Hawthorn tested the car at Silverstone. In this picture Norman Dewis tests it at the MIRA proving ground, Nuneaton. The lower photograph shows 'E2A', another 3-litre prototype, in Cunningham livery for Le Mans 1960.

The 1961 E-type's structure was a direct cross-reference from that of the 1954 D-type Le Mans car, with radiator outriggers attached to the main beam of the frame. Soon after acquisition of Daimler (1960) all the machine shops plus Jaguar's engine assembly and test facilities were transferred three miles from Browns Lane to the Radford, Coventry, works, where the XK assembly line ran clockwise, fed from adjacent sub-assembly sections.

The E-type still conjures up some of the most evocative of all automotive images, typified by this early publicity shot featuring PR man Geoff Morgan. This car dodges the number-plate problem which was to come up later. No one liked putting formal plates on the front of the E-type. Former C-type and D-type driver Max Trimble–seen (*below*) at Prescott hill-climb–might have been stopped by 'the law' and told to move his E-type's personalised plate nearer to the air intake or even have one made to fit vertically below it. The matter was never resolved fully, but most UK owners 'got away with it' if they were diplomatic.

The Ecurie Ecosse transporter, together with the 1956 Le Mans-winning car XKD 501 seen in the paddock at Oulton Park in May 1967.

Below: New in 1958 was this attractive XK150 roadster: but it was beginning to seem old-fashioned to those who had seen the first 'pre-E' prototype which was already on the road.

Norman Dewis and production prototype E-type on the MIRA banking. The E-type coupe and roadster were announced to world acclaim at the Geneva show in March 1961. Although derived directly from the D-type, they were essentially cars for the grand tour.

Below: Jaguar exhibitions man Nigel Hewin does the stunt driving for this publicity picture of the E-type.

Competition fuel-injection engines of the early 1960s. The E-type (*above*) is the dry-sumped coupé which Briggs Cunningham retained after he and Roy Salvadori had finished fourth at Le Mans in 1962.

This line-up was photographed during an employees' open day at the Browns Lane, Coventry factory in 1968. (*Below:*) Jaguar PR man James Graham with 4.2-litre E-type roadster in 1967 at Reims–scene of so many earlier successes for the marque.

The standard E-type suffered – as the XK120 had done – from *looking* like a competition car, even though it wasn't one. However, thanks to the proved reliability of the 3.8-litre XK engine, modified cars were capable of putting up an excellent performance in the GT category at Le Mans in 1962, beaten only by two Ferrari GTO's and coming fourth and fifth overall. Briggs Cunningham's coupé – seen with Bob Penney and Frank Rainbow of the Jaguar experimental department at Browns Lane, where it was prepared – was driven by the owner and by Roy Salvadori, who described it as the most comfortable competition car he had ever driven. They finished one place ahead of Peter Lumsden and Peter Sargent, whose roadster (*below*) had been turned into a fast-back coupé for the occasion.

The so-called 'lightweight' E-type of 1963 went some way towards giving Britain a competitor for the Ferrari GTO in GT racing, and Graham Hill won several races in the Coombs car (*above*). Tyres were getting wider all the time, and the same car (*below*) looked more ungainly when Jackie Stewart drove it in 1964. The only 'lightweight' car to go to Australia is seen (*below*) in the hands of Bob Jane as he wins the 1963 Australian GT Championship at Calder, near Melbourne.

This 'lightweight' E-type was one of three entered for Le Mans in 1963 by Briggs Cunningham. After an accident at Mulsanne corner, which wrecked the bonnet, it was put back into service to finish ninth. The drivers were Richards and Grossman.

(*Below:*) The low-drage coupé might have been more successful than other XK-engined E-types, but the project was dropped and the car sold to Dick Protheroe, seen in heavy traffic at Silverstone, 1964.

The most highly developed E-types were the Coombs car and the Lindner car, seen (*below*) leading the 1963 Nürburgring 100 Km *sports* car race. For 1964 this car acquired a works low-drag coupé top, but all the development in the world could not make it competitive with the Ferraris and Cobras. The alloy-block XK engine never made the grade in endurance terms. The picture (*opposite*) provided by Cecil Winby, formerly of Brico, is dated August 1964 and is captioned: 'Jaguar 3.8 litre: crown of piston hammered into three spheres–ex-Peter Lindner Lightweight E-type.' The similarity between the long-nose D-type and the E-type roadster is clearly illustrated (*bottom*).

Regular production E-types of the early and late 1960s. The 87 mm bore 3.8-litre XK engine was succeeded by the 92 mm-bore 4.2-litre version (*below*) in late 1964 for both the Mark Ten and the E-type.

Wide-angle (35°/40°) cylinder head casting (*above left*) is of petrol injection type, although Weber carburettors—as fitted to some 'lightweight' E-types—are attached for this picture. 'Lightweight' cars normally had dry-sump lubrication and Lucas fuel injection, and the highest works-recorded power output for an XK engine (April 1964) was Lindner's 344 bhp at 6500 rpm with special exhaust. The picture (*right*) may show the model for that test, but appears to feature six lenghts of Jaguar saloon heater hose!

This picture (*left*) got as far as being marked: *Confidential: Not for publication before Monday 29th March 1971.* However, it was never used. It shows how much space was under the bonnet of the fully-engineered but stillborn six-cylinder Series Three E-type, with carburettor 4.2-litre XK engine to US 'federal' specification. (Only the V-12 engine was to be offered for the production Series Three E-type.)

The last six-cylinder E-types were the Series Two two-seater roadster and fixed-head coupé, and the 2+2 coupé, built between 1968 and 1970 and recognisable by their larger air intakes and protruding headlamps. The latter was photographed by the author in the village of Clères, near Rouen, famed for its motor museum. In the lower picture, Jim Graham drives the roadster while – once again – the favourite E-type publicity shot is taken.

The majority of 'bread-and-butter' Jaguars – the saloons – from late 1950 to early 1987 were powered by the XK engine, and were vital to Jaguar's very existence. In September 1955, the marque entered a new field with the announcement of its compact '2.4' saloon to supplement the big MK VII and the XK sports-car range. It had a short-stroke (83 mm x 76.5 mm) version of the XK engine displacing 2483 cc and featuring twin downdraught Solex carburettors. These prototypes show three stages of the 2.4's development. The Browns Lane sportsfield shot (*below*) illustrates the final version, with only the parking-lamp design and position still to be settled.

The 2.4 was the first Jaguar saloon of full monocoque construction. It had the distinctive feature of rear-wheel spats—a throw-back to the XK120 and Mark Seven. For production there would be a large leaping Jaguar mascot on the bonnet.

Centre: Some eighteen months after the 2.4, in early 1957, came the inevitable 3.4, which gave Jaguar the world's fastest series-production four-door saloon. It was recognisable in profile by the cutaway wheel spats.

Below: Disc brakes were offered—really, they were essential—for the 3.4 saloon from late 1957, and the model built up a fine competition record. Here Walt Hansgen wins the 1959 US Grand Prix supporting event at Sebring. (The 3.4's wide grille was, in due course, adopted for the 2.4.)

Transfer of many departments to Radford in the early 1960s would leave Browns Lane (still Jaguar's headquarters) more space for vehicle assembly. This picture (*below*) shows the Radford production engine test shop with XK engines on the left and Daimler V-8 engines on the right soon after the move. A 2.4 engine is second from left in the foreground.

On the production line at Browns Lane the 2.4/3.4 body-cum-chassis was lowered on to a jig carrying the assembled engine, transmission and suspension units. The early 2.4's Solex carburettors cleared the main frame member as it dropped, whereas the 3.4's SUs had to be removed and refitted during this operation.

Below: In autumn 1959, the 2.4 and 3.4 were replaced by the Mk 2 range, for which the 3.8-litre engine was third alternative. With the advent of motorways, the Mk 2 was a more popular police car than ever.

The 3.8 MK 2 enjoyed four seasons of international competition success. By 1963, Ford's assault on world motor sport was being felt. Nevertheless, Bernard Consten (at Le Mans, *above)* succeeded in winning the touring car category of the *Tour de France* for the fourth year running.

The 3.4- and 3.8-litre S-type saloons (1963 to 1968) provided more interior and luggage accommodation than the Mk 2, which they supplemented, and they had all-independent suspension – but they lacked the flair and style of the Mk 2.

An improvement over the S-type's front-end styling was achieved with the 4.2-litre Jaguar 420 (1966 to 1968). Shown here (*left*) is a rare if not unique drophead coupé conversion by the London coachbuilder Harold Radford. At the same time, the Daimler Sovereign was introduced. It was the first 'Daimler' to be given the Jaguar XK engine, but it was essentially a Jaguar 420. This one (*right*) is seen outside the old Daimler works in Sandy Lane, Coventry, on the occasion of a visit by journalist and former Daimler apprentice S. C. H. ('Sammy') Davis.

The last of the compact Jaguars to remain in production was the 240 (the 'MK 2' title had been dropped), which remained on the market until well into 1969, by which time Jaguar's Jim Graham was becoming quite a star of works action photography.

The Jaguar Mark Ten, or MK X was in production from 1961 to 1970. It had a triple-carburettor XK engine which went from 3.8 to 4.2 litres in 1964. In 1966, a number of improvements (and, perhaps, poor sales?) led to a change of name: it became the 420G. The elegant 420G was comfortable and refined and paved the way for the XJ6; but it was just too bulky to sell well. However, from 1968, it provided the ideal basis for a new Daimler limousine.

Installation of the 4.2-litre XK engine in the 1986 XJ6. Cross-bracing struts have been removed for the purpose of the photograph.

Below: Distinctive 'hips'—an E-type legacy—characterized the rear wing line of the XJ6 in 1968 and would still be discernible in the 'XJ40' models twenty years later. Straight exhaust outlet pipes (pictured here) pulled in fumes, and were moved outwards later on.

Traditionally a race with a Le Mans-type start, the Silverstone international touring car event of July 1959 was given a grid start in deference to harness-wearers. Jaguar 3.4s dominated it as usual, with Walt Hansgen winning spectacularly in No. 34. For over a decade, Jaguars dominated British saloon car racing.

The 2.4 and its successors added a new dimension to Jaguar's sporting image worldwide. The early example above was fitted with Amal carburettors for racing in Australia. Compact Jaguars—like this one at Donington (*below*)—were still being raced for pleasure in the 1980s.

Mike Salmon, now better known as a driver of historic Aston Martins, at the wheel of his 3.8-litre MKII Jaguar in the Touring Car race at Silverstone in July 1963. The race was dominated by the Ford Galaxie of Jack Sears and Salmon's engine blew up in his vain pursuit of the American car. (*Guy Griffiths*)

Mike Campbell-Cole with his 3.8-litre MKII mixes it with a Mini and a Mini-Cooper in the Touring Car race at Silverstone in July 1965. He retired because of a broken fan-belt. By this time the class was dominated by the Lotus-Cortinas. (*Below:*) Caplan's 3.8-litre MKII on the start-line at Weston Speed Trials in October 1967 is the famous 'Tommy' Atkins car raced by Ray Salvadori. Both photographs are by Guy Griffiths.

The 4.2-litre XK engine as fitted to the 420G had three SU carburettors and was quoted as developing a somewhat optimistic 265 bhp. It was a great engine all the same.

The Jaguar 420 of 1966-68 was a good-looking car, but very much an interim model—awaiting the XJ6.

One of the original 1968 works 4.2-litre XJ6 saloons – an overdrive model later owned by the author. The XJ6 established the Jaguar marque strongly during Leyland's tenure, and was the company's major asset when it become independent again.

The XJ6C was announced in 1973 as part of the new Series Two range, but it was not ready for production until early 1975. The author preferred the Series Three-style lower grille for his all-white coupé (*below*) but could not 'sell' the idea at Jaguar.

Series Three XJ6 construction ran from 1979 to 1987. This model was the last volume-production car to have the XK engine. However, the famous power unit continued to be made in small quantities for the unique Daimler Limousine and for military vehicles—a situation that looked set to continue into the 1990s.

Famous 1968 photograph of Sir William Lyons and Bill Heynes with their ultimate concept–the Jaguar XJ6. Leading lieutenants to be noted in the foreground include Bob Knight, Norman Dewis, Jim Randle, Keith Graham, Tom Tones, Malcolm Sayer, Fred Gardner, Claude Baily, Gerry Beddoes, 'Doc' Tait and Ted Addy. Also in the group is Trevor Crisp–the man who leads Jaguar power unit engineering today, and who was responsible for the successful 'federalizing' of the XK engine, which was essential for Jaguar's retention of a share of the North American luxury and sports-car markets.

The Daimler Sovereign version of the XJ6 was announced in October 1969—just over a year after its Jaguar counterpart.

Below: In 1973, the Series Two XJ6 was introduced universally, although its raised bumper was brought in specifically to meet US regulations. This 1975 example was run by the Avon and Somerset Constabulary.

The XJ6 was originally announced with the alternative of 4.2- or 2.8-litre engines, the latter being a hybrid designed to meet certain continental tax categories. The 2.8 was not a commercial or a technical success, however, and in early 1975 the original 3.4-litre XK's engine dimensions returned to the catalogue for the base-model Series Two XJ6.

Below: The two-door Series Two (1973 to 1977) was a beautiful car, but the complex side-window design made it difficult to achieve the low wind noise required for a luxury car; it did not come on to the market until early 1975.

From 1972, longer-wheelbase models had been offered, and within a few years the 'short' XJ models were available only in two-door form. In 1979 the Series Two XJ6 (*top*) was replaced by the Series Three shown (*centre*) with alternative wheel trim suggestions. The Series Three had much cleaner front end styling (*below*) which would carry on into the 'XJ40' era (for V-12 models), still much admired.

The Series Three XJ6 (*below*) compared with the original SS Jaguar style first seen in the autumn of 1935. From 1978, the 4.2-litre XJ6 forsook the traditional SU carburettor set-up (retained on the 3.4) in favour of the Lucas/Bosch L-jetronic electronic fuel injection system (*left*).

Daimler's own V-8 engines, excellent as they were, had been dropped in the late 1960s, and only its famous fluted radiator grille surround identified the marque clearly–as in the XK-engined Series Three photographed at Shelsley Walsh, the ancient speed hill-climb course where Daimler starred in the first decade of the century. Although based on the Jaguar 420G (Mk X), the Daimler limousine has enabled Daimler to maintain an identity of its own. This example (*below*) is one of two landaulette versions built to special order in the 1970s.

The 4.2-litre XK-engined Daimler Limousine was introduced in June 1968 as a Jaguar exercise in conjunction with Vanden Plas, the London coachbuilders. It replaced Daimler's own Majestic Major, and utilized an extended version of the Jaguar 420G sub-structure. Production was moved to Coventry when the Vanden Plas works was closed down in the early 1980s, and a special department was set up at Jaguar's Browns Lane works. More recent versions of limousine (*below*) have neater front-end treatment than their predecessors.

In the first forty years of its existence, the XK engine has proved useful to many companies and individuals outside the Jaguar organization. The first person to succeed in persuading Bill Heynes to let him fit one in a car of his own design was Jerseyman Frank Le Gallais, whose rear-engined LGS-Jaguar was a highly professional sprint car exercise. It is seen at Bouley Bay, where Le Gallais broke the record several times, and (*below*) at Shelsley Walsh, whither the car was driven with nominal mudguards and silencers fitted.

In mid-1953 the first 'official' XK-engined non-Jaguar sports-racing car, the H.W.M., made its debut. However, private owner Oscar Moore had fitted such a unit to his own ex-works H.W.M. prototype in 1952, to replace its Alta engine. Moore scored many successes with this car, including victory in one of the heats of the last-ever Jersey road race. One of Moore's first actions was to bore the engine out to 87 mm to create a very early '3.8'. Later the car was owned by Gerry Scali of Plymouth, and at this time (the mid-1950s) Bruce Halford drove this pioneering machine at Brands Hatch. The car has been owned for most of its later life by Midlander Terry Grainger.

The XK engine has a fine record on water as well as on land. This impressive early-1950s craft, Christof von Mayenberg's *Mathea VII*, broke a number of international water speed records, mainly on the Wörthersee in Carinthia, where these pictures were taken.

The *very* first customer for a proprietary XK engine was Norman Buckley, who used it and later versions to break water speed records over many years from 1950 in a succession of *Miss Windermere* carft. *Miss Windermere III* is seen in action (*c.* 1958) and Buckley is shown (*left*) with Jaguar's Philip Weaver–superintendent of the experimental department and of the racing team.

There were several power-boat racing ventures involving XK engines in the early 1960s. These pictures taken at Cowes in 1963 show Sopwith's *Tramontana II* setting out for practice and Savundra's *Jackie S* 'dashboard'. Each of these remarkable vessels had four XK engines.

Bob Jankel was able to persuade Jaguar that his Panther J72 was a worthy recipient. A glimpse of the Surrey manufacturer's workshop is shown below. (V-12 engines were later offered by Panther, too.)

The XK and commercial vehicles. This Dennis ambulance design was commended highly by the 1968-69 Don Safety Award judging panel. It was fitted with a 2.8-litre XK engine and front-wheel drive, giving a low floor aft. However, it never went into production. (The same jury gave the top award to the new XJ6 for its combination of primary and secondary safety features.)

Another Jaguar-powered Dennis—and this one did get into the market place—was the D-series fire tender. Its engine was a 4.2-litre XK.

Still being ordered for the Alvis Scorpion family in the late 1980s, the 4.2-litre XK engine has been used in several different military applications since the 1960s. This is an early example of Scorpion light tank installation, with Solex carburettor.

Another fire appliance to use the 4.2-litre XK-engine was the H.C.B. Angus; but the full potential of this market was never realized, as insufficient examination of its special requirements was undertaken by Jaguar.

Two views of the Scorpion light tank built by Alvis Limited (*top and right*) and offered with the alternative of Perkins diesel and Jaguar XK petrol engines. *Below:* The Alvis Scorpion family of military vehicles, with right to left, the Sultan, the Samaritan, the Samson, the Spartan, the Striker and the Scimitar.

Main Jaguar Applications of XK Engines

1 3442 cc (83 mm x 106 mm)

XK120

Announced as 160 bhp £1263 two-seater roadster in October 1948, produced from 1949 to 1954 with fixed-head (£1644) and drophead (£1660) coupés added to range in 1952 and 1953 respectively. Special equipment ('M') model (180 bhp at 5750 rpm) alternative from 1952.

MARK VII

The saloon for which the XK engine was intended, announced in October 1950 and produced from 1951 to 1957. From 1955 model year (the 'Mark VIIM') nominal power went up from 160 bhp at 5000 rpm to 190 bhp at 5600 rpm. £1276 in 1951; £1711 in 1956 (all prices of UK, inc. contemporary tax).

XK120C

Better known as the C-type, this car had *c.*200 bhp to win Le Mans in 1951. The forty-odd 1952-53 production versions had twin 2-inch SU carburettors. The Le Mans-winning works version of 1953 had disc brakes and three twin-choke Weber carburettors, giving the XK engine *c.*220 bhp.

XK120C MK IV

New competition car for 1954: adopted name–D-type. Triple Weber carburettors standard. Typical outputs approximately 250 bhp (1954), and 270 bhp (1955). Best bench performance for '3.4' carburettor engine was 279 bhp at 5250 rpm in 1956–the year in which fuel injection was used by Jaguar in racing for the first time. ('XKSS' version also offered in small numbers in 1957, based on standard 250 bhp D-type.)

XK140

Updated sporting range (roadster, fixed-head and drophead coupés) from 1954 to 1957 priced from £1598 to £1741. Nominal output of 190 bhp, or 210 bhp or special equipment ('MC') model.

3.4-LITRE

Compact high-performance saloon based on '2.4' structure. Introduced early 1957; disc brakes optional within a year. Nominal bhp = 210 at 5500 rpm; price £1672 in UK.

MARK VIII

Successor to Mark VIIM, overlapping from late 1956 and lasting two years. Similar mechanical specification, with nominal 210 bhp. Price £1830 in UK.

XK150

Successor to XK140 from 1957 to 1960, with similar engine specifications. Disc brakes standard. XK150S (from 1958) cost over £2000 and had straight-port triple-SU carburettor cylinder head.

MARK 2 (3.4)

Updated version of '3.4' saloon, introduced in late 1959; further development for 1967-68 renamed '340'.

S-type (3.4)

Longer-wheelbase adaptation from Mark 2, featuring all-independent suspension (1963-68).

XJ6 (3.4)

This engine size (with the bore spacing of the 4.2) was reintroduced for the Series 2 XJ6 in 1975 and remained in production from 1979 until the mid-1980s in the Series 3

2

2483 cc
XK120C MK IV

(83 mm x 76.5 mm)
In September 1954, to try to overcome the TT race handicap system, two of the works D-types were entered with short-stroke crankshaft in a 3.5-litre block. Power was 190 bhp at 6000 rpm, using three Weber carburettors. Best result was fifth.

2.4-LITRE

Compact saloon car introduced September 1955, featuring twin Solex downdraught carburettors.

MARK 2 (2.4)

Updated version of '2.4' introduced in late 1959; further development for 1967 to 1969 period renamed '240'. Final models reverted to the more familiar Jaguar fuel system of two SU carburettors.

3

3781 cc
XK120C MK IV

(87 mm x 106 mm)
Following a lead taken by Alfred Momo for Briggs Cunningham in the USA, Jaguar developed their 3.8-litre XK engine for racing at Sebring in 1957 (the last appearance of a works D-type). A factory-prepared car of the *Ecurie Ecosse* team won Le Mans that year, using a works '3.8' fuel injection engine developing *c.*300 bhp.

MARK IX

Big saloon, 1958-61, based on Mark VIII. 220 nominal gross brake horsepower.

XK150

1959-60 alternatives to 3.4 and 3.4S engines were 3.8 and 3.8S. Regular models had two carburettors; XK150S had three SUs.

MARK 2 (3.8)

Successful compact saloon, made from 1959 to 1967. £1799 in UK.

S-type (3.8)

Larger-engined version of S-type saloon from 1963 to 1968.

E-type

New 2-seater sporting range, introduced spring 1961 with triple-SU 3.8-litre engine, quoted as 265 bhp at 5500 rpm. £2098 for roadster and £2197 for coupé in UK.

MARK X

New large saloon with triple-SU carburettors, launched autumn 1961 at £2392 in UK.

---

4 4235 cc

E-type — **(92 mm x 106 mm)**
4.2 replaced 3.8 in late 1964. Two-seaters supplemented by 2+2 coupé from 1966.

MARK X
4.2 replaced 3.8 in late 1964. Power output still quoted as 265 bhp (as for E-type).

420
S-type saloon structured with new front styling and 4.2 engine, 1966 to 1968. Daimler Sovereign version continued to 1969.

420G
Updated (but little changed) 4.2 Mark X, continued into 1970. Daimler limousine based on this model introduced in June 1968, and expected to continue into the 1990s.

XJ6 (4.2)
New saloon range announced in September 1968. Most models fitted with twin SU carburettors, but Zenith-Strombergs specified for US regulations. Series 2 versions (two- and four-door) launched five years later, followed by Series 3 (offered as four-door model only), which was produced from 1979 to 1987. Fuel injection from late 1970s. 1969 model UK price was £2254; 1987 model UK price was over £20,000 for top specification! Daimler versions included from 1969. All versions superseded from 1987 by latest AJ6-engined XJ40 models. (NB. Series 3 did continue in V-12 form only.)

---

5 2792 cc

XJ6 (2.8) — **(83 mm x 86 mm)**
This unit, introduced with the original XJ6, was intended to fit into certain European taxation scales, but proved troublesome and was phased out, to be replaced in 1975 by a long-stroke '3.4'. (Previously, *c.*3-litre XK engines had been tried in racing, to meet 1958-9 sports-car regulations. It may be coincidental that they were not satisfactory either.)

Suggested Reading

Many hundreds of thousands of words have been written on the subject of the XK engine and the vehicles into which it has been fitted. The following are among the more definitive works:

W. M. Heynes	**The Jaguar Engine**	The manuscript of this paper was received by the Institution of Mechanical Engineers on 27 Feb. 1953. A later paper by Bill Heynes ('Milestones') covered the later development of the XK engine for raing.
Montagu, Lord of Beaulieu	**Jaguar**	The original Jaguar history, researched by the late Michael Sedgwick and recently updated. First published by Cassell.
Skilleter, Paul	**Jaguar Saloon Cars, and Jaguar Sports Cars**	These cover all the Jaguar cars to be fitted with XK engines, and detailed background information on the power units themselves. Published by Foulis (Haynes).
Whyte, Andrew	**Jaguar Sports-Racing and Works Competition Cars *(two volumes).* (*Also* – Jaguar, the definitive history of a great British car.)**	These cover the Jaguar racing and rally history, including a number of reports and descriptions of individual engines and reprints of contemporary technical features, including the original *Automobile Engineer* XK feature.

NB: There are other Jaguar books by the above authors and many others, notably Chris Harvey and Philip Porter. Full lists of those available can be obtained from the specialist booksellers, who advertise regularly in automotive periodicals. Brooklands Books publish a series of books on contemporary descriptions and road-tests, mainly from *Autocar* and *The Motor.*

Footnote: The very first official XK engine specification, as printed in the XK120 preliminary leaflet, read as follows:
"ENGINE: Six cylinder 70° twin overhead camshaft 3½ litre Jaguar engine, 83 mm bore x 106 mm stroke; 3442 cc developing 160 bhp at 5000 rpm; compression ratio 7 to 1; highest grade cast iron block; cylinder head of high-tensile aluminium alloy with spherical (!) combustion chambers; aluminium alloy pistons; light alloy connecting rods (!!); forced lubrication throughout by submerged pump through Tecalemit full flow floating suction filter; twin SU horizontal carburettors with electrically controlled choke; counterweighted crankshaft, 2¾″ diameter in seven steel-backed bearings."

OKV 2
2

To Hefina

With love & all best wishes

for Christmas 1985.

Pip.

Here's Health

WHOLEFOOD BAKING

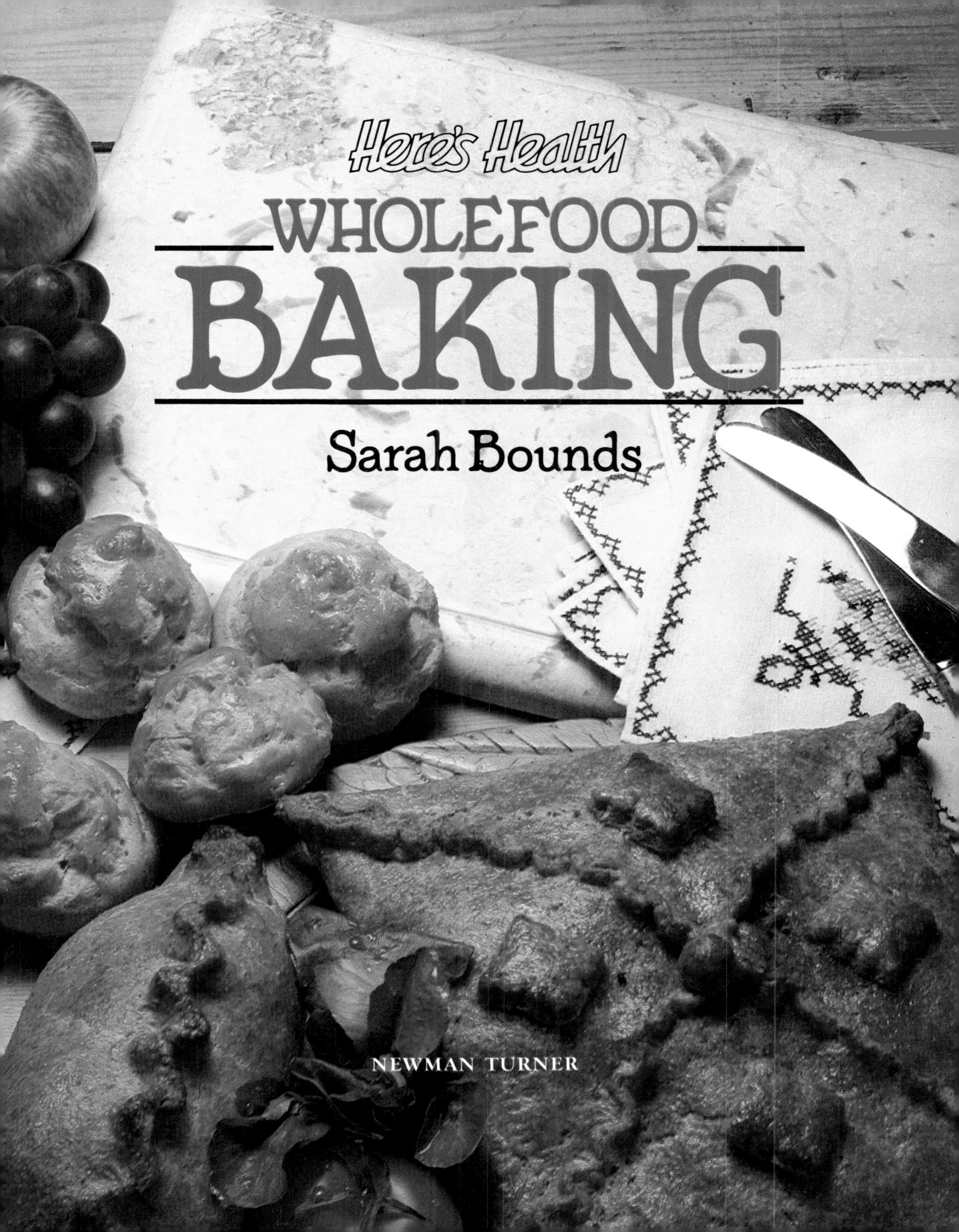
Here's Health
WHOLEFOOD
BAKING
Sarah Bounds
NEWMAN TURNER

This edition published 1984
for Newman Turner Publications Limited,
Unit 18 Goldsworth Park Trading Estate, Woking, Surrey GU21 3BJ
by Hamlyn Publishing, a division of
The Hamlyn Publishing Group Limited
Astronaut House, Feltham, Middlesex, England

ISBN 0 600 32459 1

The author and publishers would like to thank the following for the loan of accessories and equipment for photography:
Divertimenti, London SW3
David Mellor, London SW2
A Sanderson and Sons
Souleiado, London SW3

Photographs for endpapers and pages 38/39 and 88/89 were taken at the Slug and Lettuce, Winkfield, Berkshire by kind permission of the landlord.

Illustrations by Elaine Hill
Photography by Dave Jordan
Author's photograph by Graham Rye

Filmset in Monophoto Goudy
by Tameside Filmsetting Limited, Lancashire
Printed in Spain

ENDPAPERS *clockwise, from left*: Walnut Bread (page 36), Wholemeal Croissants (page 42), Coburg (page 33), Cottage (page 33), Bara Brith (page 52), Crown Loaf (page 33), Vienna (page 33), Rye Bread (page 34)

PREVIOUS PAGE *clockwise, from top left*: Crunchy Peanut Plait (page 41), Choux Pastry Buns (page 64), Ratatouille Puff (page 75), Winter Vegetable Pasties (page 66), Curried Cheese Biscuits (page 113), Oatcakes (page 111), Savoury Seed Snaps (page 111)

CONTENTS

USEFUL FACTS AND FIGURES

Notes on metrication

In this book quantities are given in metric and Imperial measures. Exact conversion from Imperial to metric measures does not usually give very convenient working quantities and so the metric measures have been rounded off into units of 25 grams. The table below shows the recommended equivalents.

Ounces	Approx g to nearest whole figure	Recommended conversion to nearest unit of 25	Ounces	Approx g to nearest whole figure	Recommended conversion to nearest unit of 25
1	28	25	11	312	300
2	57	50	12	340	350
3	85	75	13	368	375
4	113	100	14	396	400
5	142	150	15	425	425
6	170	175	16 (1 lb)	454	450
7	198	200	17	482	475
8	227	225	18	510	500
9	255	250	19	539	550
10	283	275	20 (1¼ lb)	567	575

Note: When converting quantities over 20 oz first add the appropriate figures in the centre column, then adjust to the nearest unit of 25. As a general guide, 1 kg (1000 g) equals 2.2 lb or about 2 lb 3 oz. This method of conversion gives good results in nearly all cases, although in certain pastry and cake recipes a more accurate conversion is necessary to provide a balanced recipe.

Liquid measures The millilitre has been used in this book and the following table gives a few examples.

Imperial	Approx ml to nearest whole figure	Recommended ml	Imperial	Approx ml to nearest whole figure	Recommended ml
¼ pint	142	150 ml	1 pint	567	600 ml
½ pint	283	300 ml	1½ pints	851	900 ml
¾ pint	425	450 ml	1¾ pints	992	1000 ml (1 litre)

Spoon measures All spoon measures given in this book are level unless otherwise stated.

Can sizes At present, cans are marked with the exact (usually to the nearest whole number) metric equivalent of the Imperial weight of the contents, so we have followed this practice when giving can sizes.

Oven temperatures

The table below gives recommended equivalents.

	°C	°F	Gas Mark
Very cool	110	225	¼
	120	250	½
Cool	140	275	1
	150	300	2
Moderate	160	325	3
	180	350	4
Moderately hot	190	375	5
	200	400	6
Hot	220	425	7
	230	450	8
Very hot	240	475	9

Notes for American and Australian users

In America the 8-fl oz measuring cup is used. In Australia metric measures are now used in conjunction with the standard 250-ml measuring cup. The Imperial pint, used in Britain and Australia, is 20 fl oz, while the American pint is 16 fl oz. It is important to remember that the Australian tablespoon differs from both the British and American tablespoons; the table below gives a comparison. The British standard tablespoon, which has been used throughout this book, holds 17.7 ml, the American 14.2 ml, and the Australian 20 ml. A teaspoon holds approximately 5 ml in all three countries.

British	American	Australian
1 teaspoon	1 teaspoon	1 teaspoon
1 tablespoon	1 tablespoon	1 tablespoon
2 tablespoons	3 tablespoons	2 tablespoons
3½ tablespoons	4 tablespoons	3 tablespoons
4 tablespoons	5 tablespoons	3½ tablespoons

An Imperial/American guide to solid and liquid measures

Imperial	American	Imperial	American
Solid measures		*Liquid measures*	
1 lb butter or margarine	2 cups	¼ pint liquid	⅔ cup liquid
1 lb flour	4 cups	½ pint	1¼ cups
1 lb granulated or caster sugar	2 cups	¾ pint	2 cups
1 lb icing sugar	3 cups	1 pint	2½ cups
8 oz rice	1 cup	1½ pints	3¾ cups
		2 pints	5 cups (2½ pints)

Note: When making any of the recipes in this book, only follow one set of measures as they are not interchangeable.

INTRODUCTION

Freshly baked breads and cakes, pastries and biscuits are irresistable. Their aroma is inviting and their taste rarely disappoints. But many of our traditional home-baking recipes rely heavily on white flour, sugar and fat to give lightness of texture and a sweet taste. This book aims to put that right; to present a wide selection of recipes for everything from basic wholemeal bread to Simnel cake, from gingerbread men to honey gâteau, using all natural ingredients for healthier results. Refined white flour, robbed of its dietary fibre, is replaced by wholemeal flour which retains the full goodness of the wheat and when sweeteners are added, honey, raw cane sugars and molasses are used in place of white sugar. Wherever possible the level of fat and sugar has been reduced, making these delicious wholefood alternatives a healthier bet than conventional recipes.

Wholefood baking means switching to ingredients which may be unfamiliar to many cooks. The emphasis is firmly on natural foods, which are unprocessed and unrefined so as to retain as much of the food's original nutritional value as possible. If you start with nutritious raw materials, the end product will be far healthier.

But why, when food is so plentiful in this country, need we worry about nutrients? Evidence that our diet is not as good as was once thought is now overwhelming. The National Advisory Committee on Nutrition Education (NACNE), in its report published in 1983, recommended widespread changes in our diet. In short, it concluded that the typical British diet contained too much fat, sugar and salt and too little fibre. In addition, processing of food may destroy vital vitamins and minerals which, although only needed by the body in small amounts, play key roles in maintaining health.

The typical British diet seems to explain why diseases such as heart disease, certain cancers, diabetes and high blood pressure are more common in countries in the West than they are in undeveloped nations. A high intake of fats, especially those from animal foods, is a key factor in the onset of atherosclerosis, the gradual silting up of the arteries which increases the risk of heart attacks. A high intake of fat and sugar is also likely to lead to obesity, which in itself then increases an individual's chance of developing diabetes, high blood pressure, varicose veins, heart problems, hernias and bronchitis. A lack of dietary fibre in the diet can lead to constipation, diverticulitis, colonic cancer, varicose veins and diabetes as well as be involved with heart disease.

Researchers argue that the trend in our diet to more fat and sugar and fewer carbohydrate foods such as whole cereals has emerged over the last century, as have the changes in the kinds of diseases now typical in Britain and in other Western countries. The first step to take in improving your diet is to try and reverse these dietary changes: to swop refined carbohydrates such as white bread, flour and sugar for unrefined carbohydrates such as wholemeal flour, brown rice and wholewheat pastas; to cut down on the level of fat you eat; and to switch to plant protein foods such as cereals, pulses and nuts, which provide the fibre missing from refined cereals and animal products.

In *Wholefood Baking* the recipes are based on natural wholefood ingredients to form the basis of a healthy diet; one that is nutritious, varied and acceptable to all.

Wholemeal Flour

Wheat is our staple cereal in Britain, so most of the flour used in baking is wheat flour. The wheat

Raw ingredients used in wholefood baking (see also page 21)

SPICE

grain is composed of three basic parts: the husk surrounding the grain, the wheatgerm and the endosperm. The husk or bran contains mostly dietary fibre, some protein and B vitamins. The germ, the life of the grain, contains B vitamins, vitamin E and minerals, while the endosperm mostly contains starch and protein.

The wheat grain is milled to produce flours of different extraction rates, reflecting the degree to which the original grain is retained. Standard white flour has an extraction rate of around 70 per cent. This means that 30 per cent of the grain is discarded in the milling process, leaving just the starchy endosperm, while the vitamins, minerals and fibre of the bran and germ are discarded. At the other end of the milling scale is 100 per cent wholemeal flour, where the whole of the wheat grain is retained during milling, making for maximum nutritional value. In between these two extremes is 81 or 85 per cent flour – wheatmeal flour which contains the endosperm and the germ, but little of the bran. This flour has special value in making choux pastry, which seems to be the only task which 100 per cent wholemeal flour cannot perform.

Many people unfamiliar with wholemeal flour will be surprised to learn that the flour can be used so widely in baking. Much depends, however, on the actual process used. It is important in making cakes, scones, biscuits and pastries to sift wholemeal flour first to add lightness. Not all the coarse bran particles will pass through the sieve; do not discard them, simply add them to the bowl with the flour for full nutritional value.

Wholemeal flour has more than double the level of dietary fibre, vitamins B6, folic acid, biotin and nicotinic acid; it contains four times the level of vitamin B2 and more B1, zinc, iron, magnesium and many other minerals, and it contains fewer calories than its refined white counterpart. Those new to wholemeal flour, who perhaps feel that changing over completely might be unacceptable, could start by blending half white with half wholemeal flour. Once you have tasted wholemeal flour in these baked goodies, you will never want to return to the blandness of white flour again!

Flour was traditionally milled by passing the wheat grain between stones and this basic principle still remains in use today in stonemilling. Stoneground flour tends to be expensive because the millers using this process are operating on a smaller scale than the large milling companies.The vast bulk of flour for commercial and household purposes is produced by roller milling. The industrial revolution of the last century saw the arrival of this process, which revolutionised the way British grain was milled and made possible the production of white flour on a huge commercial scale. In stonegrinding, the wheat grain is crushed between the stones, but in roller milling the rollers cut open the grain, freeing the endosperm and making it easy to split off the bran and the wheatgerm. The endosperm is then crushed to a fine white flour. Wholemeal flour can also be produced by roller milling but the bran and wheatgerm are returned to the flour once broken up.

Because the milling action of the two processes is quite different there are differences in the nature of the flour. Roller milling tends to break up the bran more finely, giving a generally finer flour than stonegrinding. The temperature generated during the roller milling process can be so high that some of the heat-sensitive vitamins, particularly the B vitamins, can be destroyed. In stonegrinding, the temperature is kept lower. Wholemeal flours are processed no further than this, while much white flour is bleached to whiten it and mature it quickly. The bleaching can further destroy B vitamins.

As well as differences in the methods of producing wholemeal flour, there are other differences to look out for when buying. Some wholemeal flours are produced from grain that is grown organically, without chemical pesticides and fertilisers. These may build up within the plant, be passed on to us and may then accumulate in our bodies to an unknown, potentially dangerous effect. Many growers are now choosing natural, organic methods of boosting productivity rather than relying on chemicals. If a product has been grown organically it will say so on the packaging, but be prepared to pay slightly more for it.

Another difference between wholemeal flours is the addition of raising agent. Wholemeal flour is available either plain (without baking powder) or as self-raising flour, to which a raising agent has been added. Throughout this book I have used plain wholemeal flour simply because it is easier to buy one type of flour and add raising agent only to those recipes that need it. Self-raising flour, on the other hand, although suitable for many cakes, scones and biscuits, is not suitable for breads, pastries or whisked sponges. If you do buy self-raising flour, simply omit the baking powder called for in some recipes.

Other Flours

While wheat is the most widely consumed cereal in Britain, there are other cereals which are important for their nutritional content. Like wheat, these cereals also lose many of their valuable nutrients through processing and refining.

As far as baking bread is concerned, it is the gluten content of a particular flour which will probably determine whether you use it or not. Gluten is required to accommodate the carbon dioxide given off during the yeast fermentation in breadmaking. Being sticky and elastic, gluten will stretch during proving processes to hold the carbon dioxide gas in even pockets. On baking, fermentation stops and the gluten sets firm, giving the risen structure of the bread. Wheat flour contains the highest level of gluten; bread made from those flours with a low gluten content does not rise as well.

Rye flour has a poor gluten content and is usually mixed with a proportion of wheat flour to make a mixed rye bread with a fairly good rise. Rye flour used alone produces a poorly risen loaf. Dark rye flour retains more of the grain's fibre than light flour.

Granary flour, a registered trade name, is made from a blend of various wheatmeal flours with malted grains. The flour is easy to use at home and produces a light loaf with a rich malted flavour and a crunchy texture. Home-made versions of Granary flour can be produced by mixing rye and wholemeal flours with cracked wheat for crunchiness.

Maize is another cereal which tends to be used in breadmaking with wholemeal flour. Corn bread, traditional in America, is made using chemical raising agents rather than yeast to produce a speedy loaf. Corn muffins are similar. Cornmeal is the name given to the flour used in baking, which contains the whole of the grain. It must be distinguished from what in Britain is called cornflour. This is simply cornstarch, refined from the grain and used to thicken liquids in cooking.

Rice is another important cereal crop. Brown rice retains the fibre, vitamins and minerals and is more nutritious than refined white rice. When rice is milled to produce a fine flour, its use is usually limited to biscuits and shortbread rather than bread as it is low in gluten.

Buckwheat flour is usually used in making pancakes. Potato flour and millet flour are also sold in health food stores; these flours are speciality products which lack the gluten needed to produce a good structure of loaf. Soya flour made from the soya bean is also available; its high protein level makes it especially useful and it is usually blended with wheat flours in baking or simply used as a thickener.

Oats

Oats deserve a special mention because they are at the centre of new research which has found that the fibre in the oat groat plays an important role in controlling the levels of cholesterol in the body. Oat fibre possesses a unique ability to reduce harmful low density forms of cholesterol which can build up as deposits on the artery walls. The arteries become narrower, work less efficiently and so reduce the flow of blood to and from the heart, increasing the risk of heart attacks. (The fibre found in wheat has little effect on blood cholesterol and works instead on speeding up the flow of material through the body's system, ensuring the fast elimination of waste products.)

Oats are used in baking either as oatmeal or as rolled oats. Fine, medium and coarse-milled oatmeals are available, and can be added to biscuits to give differing textures. Rolled oats (like the flakes of other cereals, such as barley and rye) are used in flapjacks, breads and pastry. Oatbran and oatgerm are now sold together for baking use, and can be used in biscuits, scones and muffins, mixed with flour.

Fats

In recent years there has been much coverage in the media about the fat in our diet. Supporters of margarine are quick to point out the advantages of using their product over butter and vice versa. Widespread confusion in the consumer's mind has left many totally bewildered. But one point on which there is general agreement is that we eat too much fat. Fat is the most concentrated source of calories; weight for weight, fat contains more than double the calories of proteins or carbohydrates.

Fats come in many different forms: lard, butter, margarine, vegetable oils, low-fat spreads. As far as health goes, fats are looked at from the type of their component fatty acids. Fatty acids can be saturated, unsaturated, or, if they are unsaturated in more than one place in their chemical formula, polyunsaturated. Polyunsaturated fatty acids (PUFA) include those fatty acids which are essential to the body – linoleic acid and linolenic acid. PUFA are found in fish and vegetable oils rather than in dairy fats, lard, butter and meats. PUFA have been found to lower the level of fats in the blood and this, say some researchers, has a protective effect against atherosclerosis. Others dispute the value of the PUFA action in lowering the level of fats in the blood. But it is clear that saturated and unsaturated fatty acids lack this ability and this explains why many researchers advise switching away from saturated animal fats to fats which are high in PUFA.

While PUFA are found in vegetable oils, the type of processing used to harden these oils for margarine production can saturate the fatty acids, making them useless. Look for margarines which state on the packaging that they contain a high level of PUFA – brands such as Flora and many supermarket own-label products.

Low-fat spreads such as Gold and Outline are lower in calories than conventional fats. The fat is blended with water or buttermilk to give a product that contains only half fat. They are not designed for baking use; their main value is in spreading. Lard, on the other hand, is a traditional fat which is high in saturated fats. Many conventional pastry recipes suggest using half lard and half margarine in pastry. In *Wholefood Baking* I have recommended using a soft vegetable margarine which is high in PUFA, not just in pastry making but also in cakes, biscuits and scones. There are a few recipes, however, where butter is used. The flavour of butter is hard to beat in certain recipes such as shortbread. Butter also helps to give shortness of texture and is ideal for flaky and rough puff pastries, croissants and Danish pastries. Alternatively a block margarine could be used.

Oils tend to be used more for general cooking purposes than for baking. Although shortcrust pastry can be made with oil, as can certain cakes, I find that pastry made with oil tends to be hard and lacks the fine texture of well-made shortcrust pastry. Oil is used in many of the savoury recipes in the book where ingredients need sautéing. Choose oils which have a high level of PUFA; safflower oil has the highest level but is not suitable for cooking, being best for dressings. Sunflower is second best, with corn and soya bean next. Olive oil is more stable in cooking than many vegetable oils and, although not so high in PUFA, is valued for its rich flavour.

Sugar

White sugar is excluded from wholefood cooking because it is so highly refined. It literally contains sugars and nothing else. High levels of sugar in the diet have been associated with dental caries and with obesity. Cutting down on sugar is one of the first steps to take in improving the way you eat. Where sugar is used – and this should be sparingly – it should be raw cane sugar, which has undergone less processing. Raw cane sugars contain small amounts of vitamins and minerals but these do vary. As a general rule, the paler the colour, the more the processing that has been used. Lightest of the raw cane sugar family is light Muscovado, followed by demerara, dark Muscovado and molasses sugars.

After white sugar has been refined, the residue remaining is molasses. Liquid molasses is a rich, thick, dark liquid, high in B vitamins and minerals such as iron, calcium, potassium and phosphorus. It is still sweet, however, and so not always an ideal supplement to take to get extra nutrients. In baking it imparts a rich, dark colour to breads, cakes and biscuits.

Honey is another sweetener used in wholefood cooking. It comes in many colours and varieties; cheapest are the blended products. Clear honey is easier to use for baking purposes than thick honey, because it is lighter and easier to handle. Honey contains small amounts of minerals and vitamins and is also a natural antiseptic. It imparts a delicate flavour, a golden colour and a silky texture to cakes, breads and biscuits, but use it sparingly to avoid overpowering other ingredients. Honey also makes an attractive, glossy glaze for baked goods. It does tend to burn easily, though, so take care that foods made with honey do not overbrown.

Eggs

Eggs are storehouses of nutrients for the developing chick. They also provide us with a valuable source of iron, B vitamins, vitamin E and protein, but unfortunately they contain high levels of saturated fat and cholesterol, so their consumption should be limited. Nevertheless, eggs perform valuable roles in baking. They can be whisked to incorporate lightness into cakes, they thicken and so set quiche fillings and custards, they bind pastries and biscuit doughs and are used in glazing breads to give a golden, glossy finish.

Free-range eggs have been specified in these recipes. Many people feel that the methods used in rearing battery chickens to produce eggs are inhumane and prefer instead to support farmers who produce eggs by free-range methods, where the hen has more freedom of movement. Battery systems of production often rely on chemically fortified feeds for speedy growth and these may also contain artificial dyes to produce an egg with a deeper coloured yolk.

Milk

Milk is used in varying quantities in baking to enrich doughs, to add extra moisture to cake mixtures to prevent their drying out, as well as to form the basis of many fillings for pies and quiches, both sweet and savoury.

Most milk drunk in Britain is full-fat milk and as such contains high levels of saturated fat. Increasingly, dairies are making fresh skimmed milk available for sale. Skimmed milk contains half the calories of ordinary milk because the fat has been skimmed off. In cooking it is indistinguishable from full-fat milk and using it is an easy way of controlling both your fat and calorie intake. Skimmed milk cheeses are useful in cooking, too, as they are low-calorie alternatives to full-fat cheeses.

Yogurt is another valuable ingredient and, again, is best made from skimmed rather than full-fat milk. Yogurt has a characteristically tangy taste which makes it an ideal ingredient in certain recipes to counteract any richness. Yogurt also contains bacteria which are helpful in promoting healthy digestion.

Dried Fruits

Currants, dates, sultanas, raisins, dried apricots, figs and so on are concentrated sources of fruit sugar and so tend to be used in quite high proportions in this book to cut down on the amount of refined sugars needed so that the natural foods impart their own sweetness. Dried fruits contain fibre and varying amounts of minerals and vitamins. Dried apricots are among the most nutritious, as they contain carotene, the vegetable precursor of vitamin A, and potassium.

Nuts

Nuts are used to a greater extent in wholefood than in other kinds of cooking, particularly by vegetarians who take advantage of their protein content. Nuts can be bought whole, shelled, chopped or ground. Almonds, hazelnuts and pistachios need skinning before they can be used. Almonds are blanched by putting them into a pan with water to cover and bringing them to the boil. They are then drained, run under a cold tap and the skins rubbed off. Once blanched they can be split in half or chopped or ground. A liquidiser or grinder will grind nuts to a fairly fine consistency, as will a food processor. Hazelnuts, peanuts and pistachios can all be skinned either by toasting them under a hot grill or by warming them in the oven. The skins are then simply scrubbed off the heated nuts. Walnuts, brazils and pecans do not need to be skinned.

Carob

Carob is used in wholefood baking to replace chocolate and cocoa. It comes from a bean which has been ground to a very fine powder. It is also sold in bar form as an alternative to chocolate and this can be melted and used to coat cakes, biscuits and so on.

Carob is naturally sweeter than cocoa so it doesn't need to be mixed with as much sugar in recipes as cocoa does. It is also lower in fat, hence in calories; it contains vitamins A, B and D and numerous minerals, and it is free from cocoa's oxalic acid which binds with calcium and stops the calcium from being used by the body. Chocolate is also often a source of allergies and can cause migraine in sensitive individuals. This is due to its caffeine and theobromine content, both possible allergens which also stimulate the body. Carob contains neither, making it a safer bet all round.

Seeds

Like nuts, sesame and sunflower seeds play a more important role in wholefood cooking than in conventional dishes. They are good sources of protein and contain vitamins and minerals too. Seeds add flavour and an interesting bite to baked goods, both sweet and savoury. Often they are lightly toasted before use to bring out extra flavour. This is done by spreading the seeds out in a grill pan or on a baking tray and then placing them either under a hot grill or in a hot oven for a few minutes until they start to change colour – take care not to overbrown them or they will char and be ruined.

Pulses

Beans, peas and lentils make up the family of pulses or legumes. They are useful sources of protein for vegetarians and wholefooders who wish to cut down on meat. They also contain vitamins and minerals and fewer calories than meat, being low in fat.

Dried pulses often need lengthy soaking before cooking. All dried beans, except the black eye bean, need presoaking. This can either be done overnight in cold water or by a time-saving method whereby the beans are placed in boiling water and left to stand for one hour. Lentils, fresh peas and beans do not need presoaking.

Protein in a Wholefood Diet

Nuts, seeds, pulses and grains are all used in larger amounts in wholefood than in conventional eating because they are healthier sources of protein than animal foods. They contain less fat and the fats they do supply are polyunsaturated and unsaturated rather than saturated. Important vitamins and minerals are also present.

However, care needs to be taken when eating plant proteins without animal proteins, because they do not contain such a high quality of protein. Plant foods do not individually contain all the amino acids which make up the proteins that we need at each meal, whereas animal foods do. To overcome this, it is important to combine different plant proteins for a good balance. Grains, pulses, and nuts and seeds form three distinct groups, each short of a different amino acid. By mixing two of the three groups at one meal it is possible to obtain a good balance of amino acids. Alternatively, plant proteins can be mixed with animal proteins – meat, fish, eggs, milk or cheese – to give a good amino acid balance.

Because red meats contain high levels of saturated fats and can also bear traces of antibiotics and other chemicals which may have been added to the feeds of livestock, poultry and fish make healthier alternatives. Poultry contains less fat than red meat, as does game, and the fat is polyunsaturated. Fresh fish, on the other hand, contains a type of polyunsaturated fatty acid (PUFA) that is thought beneficial in protecting against heart disease. This is found in fatty fish like mackerel and herrings. White fish are lower in calories than oily fish. Both contain vitamins and minerals too.

Key to Ingredients on Page 15

1 wheat flakes
2 oatmeal
3 rye flakes
4 millet flakes
5 wheat grains
6 wheatgerm
7 bran
8 pulses – chick peas, butter beans, flageolets and white haricot beans
9 100% wholemeal flour
10 nuts – walnuts, pecans, hazelnuts, chestnuts and peanuts
11 yeast, fresh and dried
12 dried fruits – apples, pears, peaches, apricots, prunes, figs and raisins
13 seeds – sunflower seeds and roasted and unroasted pumpkin seeds
14 honeycomb
15 jumbo oats
16 carob powder
17 milk
18 lentils
19 cinnamon sticks

THE EQUIPMENT

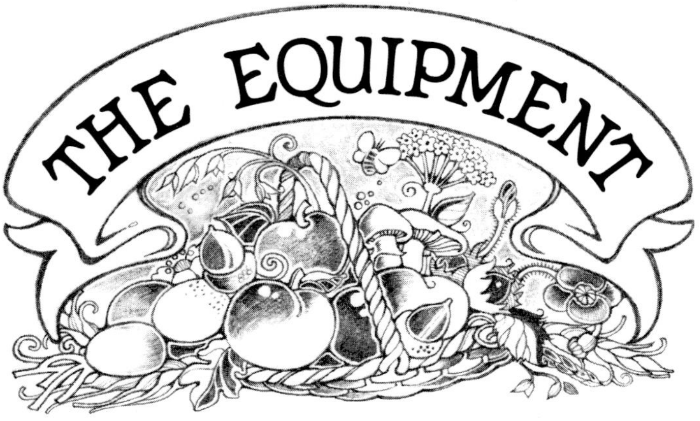

The equipment for baking at home falls into two categories – preparation and cooking utensils.

Equipment needed for preparation often comprises a cook's basic equipment, vital in any kitchen. A large mixing bowl is essential for mixing breads, cakes, scones, pastries and biscuits. Choose one that is traditionally shaped, with its rim wider than its base, so there is plenty of room for the hands to rub in, mix and knead. A large bowl also helps to ensure that the maximum amount of air is incorporated into recipes where fat and sugar or sugar and eggs are beaten together. Ensure the bowl has a sturdy base, and a rim for pouring is helpful too. You can help to stop the bowl from slipping during heavy beating by placing a damp cloth under the base; this is useful in making choux pastry where the ingredients are beaten in the saucepan, as the damp cloth helps to protect the work surface from unsightly black skid marks.

Any number of smaller bowls are invaluable for holding prepared ingredients ready for adding to a recipe. It can also be helpful to sift the dry ingredients into a smaller bowl first, simply adding them to the mixture as required.

The sieve is an essential piece of equipment for the home baker, as the sifting process helps to incorporate air into a mixture. Nylon sieves are usually used for baking. The rolling pin is another essential. Although a milk bottle will do as a make-shift rolling pin in an emergency, a properly designed rolling pin will do the job more quickly and better. Choose a rolling pin that has handles moulded to it. Those with separate handles work less well, as often you can end up rolling the handles and not the pastry. Plastic rolling pins are available, with at least one on the market that is designed to be filled with cold water so that the temperature of the pastry is kept low.

Pastry boards are sometimes used as surfaces on which to roll out pastry and handle bread doughs. This is less common today than it used to be, as Formica-style worktops are almost universally used in kitchens. These worktops are smooth, even and easy to keep clean. Marble slabs, however, are making a reappearance; although expensive, they are very efficient for pastries, as they keep cool. This is particularly good for flaky and rough puff pastries, as a hot kitchen can play havoc with the large amount of fat that must be incorporated into these pastries.

A pastry brush is invaluable for glazing the tops of pies, pasties and breads so that a nicely coloured surface is achieved during baking. It is also used to dampen the edges of pastries and doughs to help seal them during baking. A small paintbrush will do the job as well as a brush that is designed for kitchen use. Bristles are made either of nylon or natural bristle. Cutters are used for stamping out rounds of biscuits,

Top to bottom: Irish Soda Bread (page 54), James's Bread (page 37), Cheryl's Bread (in toast rack and on plate, page 37), Cornbread (page 54)

pastries and scones. A set comprising several of slightly different diameters is a good buy. Metal cutters give a cleaner cut than plastic; their edges are that much sharper. Fluted cutters are conventionally used for sweet dishes and plain edged ones for savoury. Specially shaped cutters are nice for festive occasions and are fun to use; children particularly enjoy them. A pastry wheel is another gadget which is available, but by no means essential. This is used to decorate the edges of pies, but a good result can be achieved by hand (see page 63).

Electrical gadgets may also be used in baking to save preparation time. Food processors are the ultimate in food preparation machines, being capable of performing many functions, from simple chopping, grating and shredding to whisking, beating and kneading. The capacity of the mixing bowl does vary, however; often it is too small to mix an appreciable amount in one batch. Free-standing food mixers with a range of optional attachments have been around for longer than processors. The larger models do not require holding, so the operator has two free hands, and their mixing capacity is good. Creaming together fat and sugar, whisking eggs and kneading are all performed efficiently by these larger machines. Smaller hand-held models are likely to be used for creaming and whisking. You don't have to own any of these machines, however; cake mixtures can be creamed just as well, though not as quickly, by hand, either with the help of a wooden spoon or literally with the hands! Hand-held rotary whisks are useful for whisking egg whites speedily, but a fork will do the job too.

Metal spoons are vital for folding in flour and whisked egg whites. Their fine edge knocks out the minimum of air. A tablespoon is best for this role and doubles up as a measure for honey, molasses and so on. A dessertspoon is another standard measure, as is the teaspoon. Make sure you have at least one of each of these standard pieces in your kitchen. Measuring in larger quantities is possible with kitchen scales for dry ingredients and jugs for liquids. The recipes in this book give both Imperial and metric quantities: use either one or the other throughout each recipe and do not interchange them as the results may be erratic. Most kitchen scales do come marked with both weights. Sophisticated electronic scales are available for precision measuring, while traditional balancing scales are also popular. In between the old and the new are the scales that come complete with a bowl or shallow dish for measuring in one self-contained unit.

Smaller pieces of equipment which make the cook's job easier include flexible spatulas made of rubber or plastic. These help to scrape the mixing bowl clean. Juice squeezers efficiently remove the juice from citrus fruits with the minimum of wastage, while a grater with varying hole sizes will grate cheese, nutmeg, carrot, cabbage and the rind of citrus fruits. Fine grating is essential for the more strongly flavoured ingredients, such as fruit rinds and nutmeg, which are used in small amounts in recipes. Grating cheese finely makes for its more even distribution in a dish.

Scissors are useful for chopping fresh herbs, while for larger items good quality knives are needed. A set of good quality knives is one of the basic essentials of any kitchen. Choose ones which you find comfortable to hold. Most kitchen knives have straight blades but scalloped-edged blades or serrated blades are also available. Stainless steel is the most common material, but carbon steel gives a sharper blade. Handles may be of wood or plastic.

A grinder is another useful piece of equipment, invaluable to the wholefood cook for grinding nuts. A liquidiser will do the job equally well and also produce breadcrumbs and purée vegetables, soups and fruits.

A palette knife is ideal for removing biscuits from baking trays and placing them on to wire cooling trays. It is also useful for smoothing cake mixtures level in tins before baking.

The baking equipment itself is usually made of aluminium, although stainless steel, tin and non-stick products are also available. Non-stick bakeware should mean less greasing – but do check the manufacturer's instructions on this. Other types of bakeware will need greasing for cakes and breads, while pastries and biscuits which use a higher level of fat generally do not need to be put into greased tins. Each recipe will specify whether greasing is needed. For tins that have to be greased you could use an oil well, a small reservoir of oil containing a brush; as the brush is removed the sides of the well squeeze out oil, leaving just enough to smear on the tins. The idea is to use as little oil as possible, so saving on calories. This implement will also be invaluable for sautéing ingredients.

Here is a list of the bakeware you will probably find most useful:

two 450 g/1 lb loaf tins
one 900 g/2 lb loaf tin
two 18 cm/7 in sandwich tins
one 20 cm/8 in round, deep cake tin
one 20 cm/8 in square, shallow tin
one swiss roll tin
two baking trays
one bun or tartlet (patty) tin with 12 holes
one 20 cm/8in pie plate
a set of deep pie dishes, 600 ml/1 pint, 900 ml/1½ pint and 1.15 litre/2 pint capacity
a number of 18 cm/7 in plain and fluted flan rings *or* ceramic flan dishes
wire cooling racks
one loose-bottomed cake tin (useful for cheesecakes as well as for baking)

Finally, a word about ovens. In most instances it is important to put baked goods into preheated ovens, as specified in these recipes. People with fan-assisted ovens will be aware that dishes take less time to cook and that a lower temperature can often be used. Do check with your instruction manual. As a general rule, fan-assisted ovens will cook at a temperature 10 C/50 F lower than conventional ovens. This is because heat circulation is more efficient. In conventional ovens care needs to be taken in placing items in the correct oven position; with a fan oven this is not necessary as the distribution of heat cooks food at the bottom as quickly as the food at the top. This is an invaluable asset when batch-baking foods.

The smell of freshly baked bread wafting from the kitchen is one of the most welcoming and homely of smells. The taste of home-baked bread also surpasses that of shop-bought, but many people lack the confidence to try baking their own. Apart from the money that can be saved, it does seem a little odd that, considering that bread is one of our staple foods as a nation, most of us cannot apparently bake our own and must rely on the commercial bakeries to do the job for us.

Wholemeal bread has become increasingly popular in the past few years as more and more people have become aware of the importance of fibre in their diet. But wholemeal bread provides more than just the missing fibre of white bread; it supplies extra vitamins and minerals that are simply discarded in the refining of white flour. Many people who have been weaned on to wholemeal bread from the big bakeries find their own efforts rather disappointing. This is because certain improvers are permitted in commercial wholemeal bread and in wheatmeal and brown breads. These improvers give lighter results than the inexperienced cook can hope to achieve first time.

In this first recipe chapter in *Wholefood Baking* I have based my bread recipes on the time-saving method which incorporates vitamin C. This process adds the vitamin not because of its importance to health, but because through its action as a natural dough improver, it can halve the time needed for making bread. The result is a method which is easy to follow and which gives a light loaf – one that all the family will find acceptable.

The Steps in Bread Making

A loaf of bread is produced by the action of yeast on flour in the presence of water, salt and possibly fat. The golden rules of bread making have been formulated around the needs of the yeast cells; too hot a temperature kills off the yeast before it has had time to work and too cool a temperature slows down its activity. The ideal temperature at which yeast works is 25C/78F so the environment in which the dough is left to rise should be around this temperature. Anything above 54C/130F will kill the yeast.

In bread making, yeast ferments in the presence of starches in the flour to produce carbon dioxide. The gas is collected within the framework of the dough to produce a risen structure. The dough doubles in size, made possible by the presence of gluten in wheat flour. Gluten is produced when two of the proteins in wheat are kneaded with water; it is an elastic substance which stretches to accommodate all the carbon dioxide. On baking in a hot oven, the

Clockwise, from left: Malt Loaf (page 55), Spiced Honey Bread (page 55), Swedish Tea Ring (page 52), Chelsea Buns (page 48)

yeast is killed and the gluten is set to a firm structure – the nice, even texture of a loaf.

To achieve this result there are several steps in conventional bread making:

1. Activating the yeast: the yeast is mixed with the water (or milk) which has been heated to a temperature of about 40C/105F. The warm liquid combined with cold yeast produces the right temperature to activate the yeast.

2. Mixing the dough: the yeast liquid is poured on to the flour and the dough is produced by mixing the liquid thoroughly into the flour.

3. Kneading: this process develops the gluten in the flour and distributes the yeast throughout the dough evenly.

4. Rising: the dough is covered and left to double in size.

5. Knocking back and shaping: the risen dough is kneaded again and becomes deflated. It is then shaped.

6. Proving: the dough is covered and left in a warm place to double in size once again.

7. Baking: the risen dough is baked in a hot oven.

Although the aims are the same, the short-time method of bread making cuts out the initial rising process, replacing it with a resting period of ten minutes. The dough is then left to double in size and is baked. These steps will be considered in detail, but first let's look at the basic ingredients of bread making.

Flour

For wholefood baking the basic flour is wholemeal, made from the whole of the wheat grain. (This can be either stoneground or roller-milled, see page 16). Flours for bread making are traditionally produced from wheats selected for their high gluten content, helping to produce a better risen loaf. Our climate is not suited to these so-called strong wheats. Canadian wheats are imported specifically for their strength. Many of the wholemeal flours on the market, particularly those produced by smaller mills, are home-grown, which means they are made from soft, comparatively low-gluten English wheats. Flours produced from organically grown wheats are more likely to be home-grown, too. Other bigger company brands of wholemeal flour are more likely to blend English wheats with harder Canadian wheats.

It is impossible to know when you are buying whether you are getting a flour ideal for bread making or not; with white flour at least there is a distinction made, as strong white flour is specifically designed for bread making. The likelihood that wholemeal flours are softer is another reason for using the time-saving bread making recipe, as these flours actually benefit from a shorter bread making method. As with its commercial counterpart, the Chorleywood process, softer, low-gluten flours can be used. The Chorleywood process also uses vitamin C and combines higher proportions of yeast and fat, reducing proving time by employing intense mechanical handling. Although at home this last factor is not possible, it is important to knead the dough thoroughly.

Other Flours

Wheat flour is generally used in bread making because of its high gluten content. It is difficult to produce nicely risen loaves from low-gluten flours such as maize, rye, rice, oats and so on, using the conventional bread making process. Cornmeal is used in baking quickbreads which rely on chemical raising agents. Rye is usually mixed with wheat flour to produce a loaf which rises slightly. Oatmeal or rolled oats are added to a standard wheat dough to give added texture and flavour. Rice flour is exceptionally fine and not suitable, although cooked rice grains can be mixed into the dough to give a moist, satisfying loaf. Soya flour, which is high in protein, can be added in a small quantity to dough to boost the protein level. One other flour often used in bread making is Granary flour, made from a blend of wheatmeal, rye and malted grains to produce a distinctive tasting loaf.

Yeast

Baker's yeast is produced in huge quantities from molasses by just a few companies in Britain. Fresh yeast is sold in health food stores and by some bakers, usually small independent ones.

Fresh yeast should be pale, creamy beige in colour and preferably in one piece; if it is crumbly it is likely to be stale. Fresh yeast will keep for up to a week, wrapped in cling-film in the refrigerator. Alternatively, freeze it and store it for up to 3 months. Pack yeast for the freezer in 15 g/½ oz blocks. In an emergency, frozen yeast can be used straight from the freezer; simply add it to the tepid water and give it a few minutes longer to come back to life before pouring the mixture on to the flour.

Many people believe it is necessary to add sugar to the yeast but this is unnecessary. The starches in flour are broken down and are adequate food for the yeast cells.

As a basic guide to how much yeast to use, 15 g/½ oz will rise up to 450 g/1 lb flour and 25 g/1 oz up to 1.4 kg/3 lb. These amounts are higher than in some recipes, but the fast method does need slightly more yeast.

Dried yeast is a convenient alternative to fresh yeast. Remember to halve the quantity of fresh yeast called for in the recipe, but check with the packet instructions too. Dried yeast needs to be activated for a longer period of time. This is also an indication of whether the yeast is still alive – very old dried yeast becomes inactive. Take one third of the amount of water required in the recipe and sprinkle the yeast on top. Leave to froth, then add the mixture to the flour with the remaining liquid and proceed as normal. The operation of dried yeast is also assisted if the flour is warmed first – but don't overheat it.

New arrivals on the market are dried yeasts which can be added straight to the flour. These autolysed yeasts are more powerful than standard dried yeasts, but follow the packet instructions carefully.

Liquid

For plain breads, water is added to moisten the dough and to produce gluten from the wheat proteins. The water temperature should be 36–37 C/98–100 F, and no hotter than 43 C/108 F. The warm liquid combined with cold yeast produces the right temperature to activate the yeast.

Milk is sometimes used for a soft-textured loaf. Baps can be produced by mixing half water and half milk. Sweet, enriched doughs benefit by the addition of milk and beaten egg to give a soft crumb. Buttermilk is another liquid used in some bread making. It is the fluid left after butter making and is slightly acidic. It is ideally suited to scones and soda breads where it assists the action of chemical raising agents.

Fat

The basic bread doughs in this book contain added fat as this helps the time-saving method. For the sake of economy this is usually a margarine, but one high in PUFA. Where flavour and texture are important, for instance in croissants and Danish pastries, butter is specified; a hard margarine would give the correct texture but the flavour would be lacking!

Oil can be used in bread making. For the pizza dough choose a superior quality, cold-pressed olive oil. For other doughs, 2 teaspoons of oil could replace the margarine.

Salt

Salt is added to bread to give flavour. It also strengthens the gluten in dough: this is vital to the commercial baker, who will add a precise measure of salt, but home baking seems to be

little affected by its omission. The matter of taste however is different and highly personal. Having written *No Salt Cookery*, I have found that I can quite happily bake and eat bread without a grain of salt. Visitors, though, do notice the omission, so as a concession I tend to mix in about half the normal amount. This amounts to 1 teaspoon salt per 675 g/$1\frac{1}{2}$ lb quantity of dough. In sweet dough I leave the salt out altogether and have yet to receive complaints. Trying to cut down on the amount of salt in the diet is quite important, especially if you or any of your family suffer from high blood pressure. Using unsalted butter when necessary can help to achieve this end.

Spices and Flavourings

Spices such as nutmeg, allspice and cinnamon are traditionally added to sweet recipes, either individually or as mixed spice blends. They can be sprinkled into the flour at the onset or kneaded thoroughly into the rested dough. Savoury spices and herbs, grated orange and lemon rind and finely chopped onion and garlic will all give bread extra flavour; this is particularly useful where the level of salt is being reduced.

Sugar

Although yeast works happily without the addition of sugar, some breads do benefit in other ways from extra sweetness. Molasses gives rye bread its characteristic dark colour, and sweet doughs are usually sweetened with additional sugar. In these recipes I have substituted honey for granulated sugar to give a soft crumb and a subtle hint of flavour. Glazing with a little honey mixed with warm water is another way of adding sweetness without too many calories; this gives a rich sheen to the outside of buns and loaves. Malt extract is another form of sweetener which lends a characteristic richness to the dough.

Dried Fruits and Nuts

Sultanas, currants, raisins, prunes and apricots all give flavour and natural sweetness to dough, helping to keep down the level of sweetener needed, while nuts enliven the taste and texture of all kinds of dough.

To Store Bread

Wrap bread in polythene bags or store it in an air-tight container. Bread goes stale by losing its moisture into the air, so any dry atmosphere such as the refrigerator will speed up the staling process. Home-made wholemeal bread will not stay fresh for as long as commercially baked bread and is really at its best on the day it is baked. Bread freezes well, sealed in strong plastic bags. Alternatively, uncooked dough can be frozen for future baking: place the kneaded dough in strong bags, leaving a little space for expansion, then seal and freeze. Thaw for several hours before baking.

Top: Sultana Swirls (page 50); *bottom*: Danish Pastries (page 50)

Basic Wholemeal Bread

Illustrated on pages 38–39

Makes two 450 g/1 lb loaves or 20 rolls

675 g/1½ lb wholemeal flour
½–1 teaspoon sea salt
25 g/1 oz soft vegetable margarine
25 g/1 oz fresh yeast
450 ml/¾ pint tepid water
1 (25-mg) vitamin C tablet, crushed

beaten free-range egg or skimmed milk to glaze
sesame, caraway or poppy seeds, cracked wheat or oatmeal for sprinkling (optional)

Mix the flour with the salt and rub in the margarine with your fingertips, lifting the mixture as you do so.

Crumble the yeast between your fingers into the warm water and add the crushed vitamin C tablet. Stir the mixture until thoroughly combined.

Pour the yeast liquid on to the flour and mix it in with your hands, drawing the dough together. Different flours have varying absorbencies, so you may need to add more water; alternatively, a little extra flour may be needed to stop the dough from becoming too moist. Add any extra water or flour gradually, one tablespoon at a time.

Turn the dough on to a lightly floured surface and knead it well. The kneading process is important in distributing the yeast evenly throughout the dough and in developing the gluten. Knead the dough, folding it towards you and then pushing down and away with the palm of the hand. Give it a quarter turn and continue, developing a rocking rhythm. Add a little extra flour if necessary, to prevent the dough becoming sticky; continue kneading for about 10 minutes. The dough should feel firm, smooth and elastic.

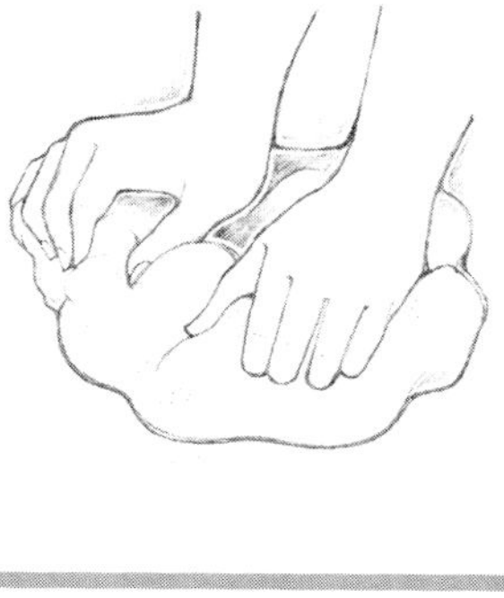

Cover the dough either with the upturned mixing bowl or with lightly greased polythene. Leave it to rest for 10 minutes. Meanwhile grease two 450 g/1 lb loaf tins or, if you are making rolls, two baking trays. Preheat the oven to hot (230 C, 450 F, gas 8).

Divide the dough into two portions and shape them. Gently pull each portion into a rectangle three times the width of the tin. Fold it into three and place it in the greased tin with the seam underneath. Alternatively, simply make two shaped loaves or 20 rolls (see page 33).

Place the tins in a warm place and cover them with a damp towel or greased polythene. This stops a skin from forming on top of the dough. Leave the bread to prove until it has doubled in size and springs back when touched with the fingertips (30–40 minutes for loaves, 20–25 minutes for rolls). Do not overprove the dough, as it can lose its elasticity and not rise fully.

Glaze the loaves with beaten egg or skimmed milk and, if liked, sprinkle seeds, cracked wheat or oatmeal on top. Beaten egg gives the glossiest, most golden finish; alternatively a milk or even a water glaze will produce a crusty top. The water glaze will be more effective if you put a pan of hot water in the oven with the bread. For a softer crust sprinkle flour on top.

Bake loaves near the top of the oven for 30–40 minutes, rolls at the very top for 15–20 minutes, until well-risen and golden brown. To test if the bread is ready, tip the loaves out of their tins and tap the bases; they should sound hollow. Cool on wire trays.

Shapes of Bread

Bread can be shaped and baked in many different ways.

Flowerpots

Choose traditional terracotta pots. Brush the insides and outsides with oil and bake them for half an hour at a high oven temperature. The pots will now be ready for baking use. Shape the dough to fit inside them, leave to prove and bake.

Cottage

Divide the rested dough into two pieces, one twice as big as the other. Shape each into a round and place the larger round on a lightly greased baking tray. Place the smaller round on top. Dip a finger into some flour and press your finger into the centre of the dough to make an indentation. Leave to prove then bake

Crown Loaf

Divide 225 g/8 oz dough into seven equal pieces. Shape each into a round and arrange six around the inside rim of a greased 18 cm/7 in sandwich tin. Place the seventh in the centre. Leave to prove, then bake.

Plait

Divide the rested dough into three equal portions. Roll each into a sausage about 30 cm/12 in long, or half as long if you are making individual rolls. Lay them side by side on the work top, pinch the top three ends together and plait them loosely. Tuck in the bottom ends and transfer the plait to a lightly greased baking tray. Leave to prove then bake.

Vienna

Shape the dough into an oval and leave it to prove. When ready, cut diagonal slashes across the top and bake.

Coburg

Shape the dough into a round and leave it to prove. When ready, slash a cross on top of the dough. The cuts should open out slightly during baking.

Individual Rolls

Rolls can be shaped in many ways. You can make smaller versions of any of the breads described previously, or make spirals or knots, as described below.

Spirals

Roll each portion of dough into a long sausage, then roll up the sausages as spirals.

Knots

Roll each portion of dough into a long sausage and tie the sausage loosely into a knot.

Rye Bread

Illustrated on pages 38–39

Makes one 450 g/1 lb loaf

175 g/6 oz rye flour
175 g/6 oz wholemeal flour
¼ teaspoon sea salt
15 g/½ oz fresh yeast
1 (25-mg) vitamin C tablet
200 ml/7 fl oz tepid water
1 teaspoon oil
1 tablespoon molasses
milk to glaze
1 tablespoon rye flakes

Put the rye and wholemeal flours into a mixing bowl and add the salt. Dissolve the yeast and crushed vitamin C tablet in the tepid water and stir in the oil and molasses. Pour the liquid on to the flour and mix to a soft but not sticky dough with your hands. If the dough is too moist, add a little extra wholemeal flour. Knead until smooth, about 8–10 minutes, cover the dough with the upturned mixing bowl and leave it to rest for about 10 minutes.

Set the oven at hot (230 C, 450 F, gas 8). Lightly grease a 450 g/1 lb loaf tin. Knead the dough lightly and shape it into a rectangle three times the width of the tin. Fold this into three and place it in the tin with the seam underneath. Cover and leave the bread in a warm place to rise for 35 minutes, until it springs back when touched with the fingertip. Glaze the loaf with the milk and sprinkle rye flakes on top. Bake it in the centre of the oven for 25–30 minutes, until it sounds hollow when tapped underneath.

Crunchy Granary Loaf

Illustrated on pages 88–89

Makes one 900 g/2 lb loaf

225 g/8 oz Granary flour
175 g/6 oz wholemeal flour
50 g/2 oz oatmeal
25 g/1 oz fresh yeast
1 (25-mg) vitamin C tablet
1 teaspoon clear honey
1 teaspoon oil
300 ml/½ pint tepid water
skimmed milk to glaze

Mix the flours and the oatmeal together in a bowl. Crumble the yeast into a jug and add the crushed vitamin C tablet, the honey, oil and water. Stir the mixture together and when the yeast has dissolved, pour it on to the flour. Mix everything together with your hands to form a soft but not sticky dough. Knead the dough on a lightly floured surface for 10 minutes, until smooth, cover it with the upturned bowl and leave it to rest for 10 minutes.

Lightly grease a 900 g/2 lb loaf tin. When the dough is ready, shape it into an oblong three times as wide as the tin. Fold this into three and drop it into the tin. Cover and leave the dough in a warm place until it has doubled in size. This will take about 30–40 minutes.

Set the oven at hot (230 C, 450 F, gas 8). Glaze the top of the loaf with a little skimmed milk and bake it in the preheated oven for 25–30 minutes, until it is golden brown and sounds hollow when tapped. Leave it to cool.

Top: Cheesy Leek Gougère (page 77); *bottom*: Honey Custard Tart (page 81)

Orange Date Teabread

8ozs chopped dates
3ozs soft margarine
1 tablespoon honey
2 ozs raw cane sugar
1 ~~orgone~~ orange grated rind & juice
6ozs SR wholemeal flour
2 tablespoon ground cinnamon
1 egg.

Place dates in saucepan with margarine, honey, sugar, orange rind & juice. Heat gently until margarine has melted. Sieve flour with cinnamon & add to mixture with egg. Beat well spread evenly in greased loaf tin. Bake at 325 gas 3 for 1¼ hrs.

Cit Jeu

Walnut Bread

Illustrated on pages 38–39

225 g/8 oz wholemeal flour
50 g/2 oz walnuts
½ teaspoon mustard powder
pinch of sea salt
15 g/½ oz soft vegetable margarine
150 ml/¼ pint tepid water
15 g/½ oz fresh yeast
1 (25-mg) vitamin C tablet
1 teaspoon clear honey
skimmed milk to glaze

Place the flour in a bowl. Chop the walnuts finely and add them to the flour with the mustard and salt. Rub in the margarine. Mix together the tepid water, yeast, vitamin C and honey and stir until the yeast has dissolved. Pour the mixture on to the flour and bring everything together to form a soft but not sticky dough. Turn this on to a lightly floured surface and knead it until smooth, about 5–8 minutes. Cover the dough with an upturned bowl and leave it to rest for about 10 minutes.

Lightly grease a baking sheet and set the oven at hot (230 C, 450 F, gas 8). Divide the dough into three. Roll each third into a fine strip, about 30 cm/12 in long. Join the three together at one end and loosely plait the strips. Lift the plait on to the baking tray, cover it with a damp tea towel and leave it in a warm place to double in size (this will take about 25–30 minutes). Glaze the loaf with milk and bake it at the top of the oven for 25–30 minutes, until it is golden brown and sounds hollow when tapped underneath. Leave it to cool on a wire cooling tray.

Grant Loaf

This recipe was developed by Doris Grant, a campaigner for food reform principles.

450 g/1 lb wholemeal flour
1 teaspoon sea salt
15 g/½ oz fresh yeast
1 teaspoon honey or molasses
400 ml/14 fl oz tepid water

Mix the flour with the salt. Stir the yeast and the honey or molasses into 150 ml/¼ pint of the water and leave to froth for 10 minutes. Pour the mixture on to the flour with the remaining water and mix well with your hands for 1 minute, until the dough feels elastic and leaves the side of the bowl clean.

Set the oven at moderately hot (200 C, 400 F, gas 6). Place the dough in a greased 900 g/2 lb loaf tin, cover and leave it to prove in a warm place for about 20 minutes. Bake the loaf in the oven for 35–40 minutes.

Many keen wholefood cooks have their own tried and tested recipes for wholemeal bread. The two that follow – James's Bread and Cheryl's Bread – are both from friends.

James's Bread

Illustrated on page 23

Makes one large loaf

450 g/1 lb wholemeal flour
25 g/1 oz wheatgerm
25 g/1 oz bran
1–2 teaspoons sea salt
1 tablespoon Muscovado sugar
500 ml/17 fl oz tepid water
1 tablespoon dried yeast

Put the flour, wheatgerm, bran and salt in a large mixing bowl and mix them together. Place the sugar and water in a jug and slowly stir in the dried yeast. Cover with a cloth and stand the jug in a warm place for 15–20 minutes, until frothy. Pour the yeast liquid on to the flour and mix it in with your hands. The dough should be tacky but not wet. Transfer the dough to a greased 900 g/2 lb loaf tin and leave it to prove in a warm place for about 20–25 minutes, until doubled in size.

Set the oven at moderately hot (200 C, 400 F, gas 6) and bake the bread for 40 minutes. Turn the loaf out of the tin and leave it to cool on a wire cooling tray.

Cheryl's Bread

Illustrated on page 23

Makes one large loaf

350 g/12 oz wholemeal flour
350 g/12 oz Granary flour
50 g/2 oz rye flour
50 g/2 oz wheatgerm
50 g/2 oz rye flakes
50 g/2 oz wheat flakes
50 g/2 oz oat flakes
50 g/2 oz millet flakes
pinch of sea salt
25 g/1 oz soft vegetable margarine
300 ml/½ pint tepid apple juice
200 ml/7 fl oz tepid water
50 g/2 oz fresh yeast
1 tablespoon molasses
1 free-range egg, beaten

Mix together all the dry ingredients and rub in the margarine. Leave the bowl in a warm place to warm gently – do not let it overheat. Mix the apple juice and water together, dissolve the yeast in the liquid and stir in the molasses. Pour the mixture into the dry ingredients and add the egg. Mix everything to a dough with your hands, turn it out on to a lightly floured surface and knead it for 10 minutes. Transfer the dough to a lightly greased, 1.75 kg/4 lb loaf tin, or two 900 g/2 lb tins, cover with a damp cloth and leave in a warm place for 1 hour to double in size.

Set the oven at moderately hot (190 C, 375 F, gas 5). Place the loaf in the centre of the oven and bake it for 35–45 minutes until it sounds hollow when tipped out of the tin and tapped underneath. Leave the bread to cool on a wire cooling tray.

OVERLEAF *clockwise, from left*: Crown Loaf (page 33), Wholemeal Croissants (page 42), Plait, Coburg and Cottage (page 33), Bara Brith (page 52), Hot Cross Buns (page 47), Banana and Hazelnut Bread (page 55), Vienna (page 33), Rye Bread (page 34), Walnut Bread (page 36)

Cheese and Mushroom Plait

Illustrated on pages 60–61

Serves 3

225 g/8 oz wholemeal flour
pinch of sea salt
15 g/½ oz fresh yeast
1 (25-mg) vitamin C tablet
150 ml/¼ pint tepid water
1 teaspoon oil
FILLING
1 teaspoon oil
50 g/2 oz onion, finely chopped
100 g/4 oz button mushrooms, finely chopped
½ teaspoon dried thyme
freshly ground black pepper
75 g/3 oz Double Gloucester cheese, finely grated
beaten egg to glaze

Put the flour and salt in a mixing bowl. Place the yeast and crushed vitamin C tablet in a jug and pour in the tepid water. Stir until the yeast has dissolved, then add the oil and pour the liquid on to the flour. Bring the dough together, using your hands, turn it on to a lightly floured surface and knead it for about 5 minutes, until smooth. Cover with the upturned bowl and leave the dough to rest for 10 minutes.

Meanwhile, prepare the filling. Heat the oil and cook the chopped onion gently in it for 2 minutes. Stir in the chopped mushrooms and the thyme and cook for a further 2 minutes. Season with black pepper.

Lightly grease a baking tray. Roll the dough out to a 25 × 20 cm/10 × 8 in rectangle and place this on the baking tray. Arrange the mushroom mixture down the centre to within 1 cm/½ in of the top and bottom of the rectangle and 6 cm/2½ in of each side. Top the filling with all but 15 g/½ oz of the cheese. Make diagonal cuts down the free sides of the dough at 2.5 cm/1 in intervals and dampen the edges. Starting at the top, fold down the top piece of the dough and then alternately bring a strip from each side over the filling to meet in the centre. Fold up the bottom piece. Cover and leave the plait to prove in a warm place for 20 minutes.

Set the oven at hot (220 C, 425 F, gas 7). Glaze the plait with beaten egg and sprinkle the remaining cheese on top. Bake it at the top of the oven for 20–25 minutes, until firm and golden brown. Serve hot.

Crunchy Peanut Plait

Illustrated on pages 104–105

Cuts into 10 chunky slices

350 g/12 oz wholemeal flour
50 g/2 oz crunchy peanut butter
15 g/½ oz fresh yeast
1 (25-mg) vitamin C tablet
1 teaspoon Muscovado sugar
250 ml/8 fl oz tepid water
skimmed milk to glaze
1 tablespoon chopped roasted, salted peanuts

Put the flour in a bowl and rub in the peanut butter. Mix together the yeast, crushed vitamin C tablet, sugar and water and stir until the yeast has dissolved. Pour the yeast liquid on to the flour and mix everything to a dough with your hands. Turn the dough on to a lightly floured surface and knead it for 5–8 minutes, until smooth. Cover it with the upturned bowl and leave it to rest for 10 minutes.

Lightly grease a baking tray. Set the oven at hot (230 C, 450 F, gas 8). Divide the dough into three and roll each third out to a strip about 38 cm/15 in long. Join the three strips at one end and plait them loosely together. Place the plait on the baking tray, cover and leave it in a warm place for about 30 minutes, until doubled in size. Glaze the plait with milk and scatter chopped peanuts on top. Bake it in the centre of the oven for 25–30 minutes, until it is golden brown and sounds hollow when tapped underneath. Leave it to cool on a wire cooling tray.

Cheese and Garlic Crown

Illustrated on pages 104–105

Serves 7

225 g/8 oz wholemeal flour
100 g/4 oz farmhouse Cheddar cheese, finely grated
1 clove garlic, crushed
15 g/½ oz fresh yeast
1 (25-mg) vitamin C tablet
150 ml/¼ pint tepid water
skimmed milk and sesame seeds to glaze

Place the flour in a bowl and mix in the cheese and garlic. Crumble the yeast, crush the vitamin C tablet and add them both to the water. Stir until the yeast has dissolved, then pour the liquid into the bowl. Mix everything together with your hands to form a soft but not sticky dough; you may need to add extra flour. Turn the dough out on to a lightly floured surface and knead it for 5–8 minutes, until smooth. Cover it with the upturned mixing bowl and leave it to rest for about 10 minutes.

Set the oven at hot (230 C, 450 F, gas 8). Lightly grease an 18 cm/7 in sandwich tin. Divide the dough into seven equal pieces, roll each into a ball and arrange six around the inside rim of the tin. Place the seventh in the centre. Cover and leave the crown in a warm place to double in size (this will take about 20 minutes). Glaze it with milk, sprinkle sesame seeds on top and bake the crown at the top of the oven for 15–20 minutes. Serve hot.

Herb Roll

Illustrated on pages 72–73

Serves 8

225 g/8 oz wholemeal flour
1 tablespoon sesame seeds
15 g/$\frac{1}{2}$ oz fresh yeast
1 (25-mg) vitamin C tablet
150 ml/$\frac{1}{4}$ pint tepid water
1 tablespoon oil
2 cloves garlic, crushed
50 g/2 oz onion, finely chopped
1 tablespoon chopped fresh parsley
1 teaspoon fresh or $\frac{1}{2}$ teaspoon dried thyme
freshly ground black pepper
beaten free-range egg to glaze

Put the flour and sesame seeds in a bowl. Dissolve the yeast and vitamin C in the tepid water and stir in half the oil. Pour the mixture on to the flour and, using your hands, draw everything together to form a soft dough. Turn this on to a lightly floured surface and knead it for 5 minutes. Cover it with the upturned bowl and leave it to rest for 10 minutes.

Now prepare the filling. Heat the remaining oil in a pan and sauté the garlic and onion for a few minutes without letting them brown. Stir in the herbs and pepper and leave the mixture on one side.

Set the oven at hot (230 C, 450 F, gas 8). Lightly grease a baking tray. Roll the rested dough out to a rectangle measuring 30 × 20 cm/12 × 8 in. Spread the filling evenly over it and roll it up from the longest side, like a swiss roll. Cover and leave the roll to double in size (20–25 minutes). Glaze the top with beaten egg, bake it for 20 minutes and serve hot, cut into slices.

Wholemeal Croissants

Illustrated on pages 38–39

Makes 24

These are lower in fat and quicker to make than traditional recipes.

225 g/8 oz unsalted butter
25 g/1 oz fresh yeast
300 ml/$\frac{1}{2}$ pint tepid skimmed milk
6 tablespoons tepid water
1 teaspoon clear honey
350 g/12 oz Granary flour and 225 g/8 oz wholemeal flour, or 575 g/1$\frac{1}{4}$ lb wholemeal flour
1 teaspoon sea salt
top of the milk to glaze

Melt and cool 50 g/2 oz of the butter. Crumble the yeast into a jug and mix it with the tepid milk and water. Stir in the honey and melted butter and leave the mixture to stand while you prepare the dry ingredients.

Rub the remaining butter into the flours and salt until the mixture resembles fine bread-crumbs. Make a well in the centre and mix in the yeast liquid, forming a wet dough. Cover and leave to stand for about 1 hour, until the dough has doubled in size.

Set the oven at hot (220 C, 425 F, gas 7). Divide the dough into three portions (if you like you could use one portion now and freeze the other two for later). Roll each portion out to a round about 25 cm/10 in. in diameter. Cut the round into eight segments and roll each segment up

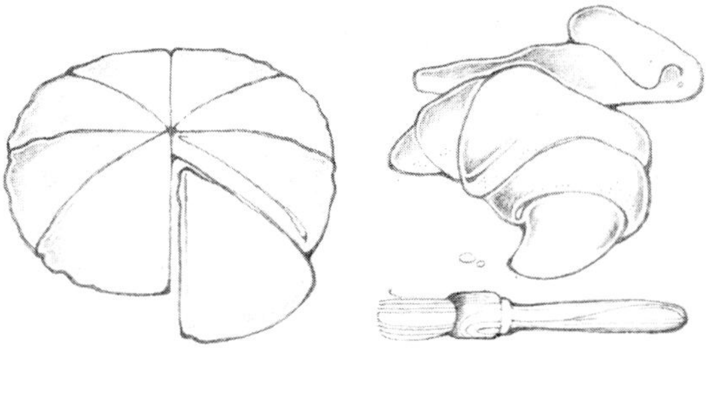

from the curved side. Moisten the points with a little water to stick and curve the rolls to form crescent shapes. Place the croissants on a lightly greased baking sheet, cover and leave them to double in size (20–25 minutes). Glaze them with top of the milk and bake them for 25 minutes, until golden brown. Serve them hot with butter and honey.

Pitta Bread

Illustrated on pages 88–89

Makes 6

The important thing to remember when making pitta bread is that it must be baked at the top of a hot oven. Unless you have a fan oven where the distribution of heat is even throughout, it is best to bake the bread in two batches, putting one half of the dough in the refrigerator while the pitta breads made from the other half are proving.

350 g/12 oz wholemeal flour
1 teaspoon sea salt
25 g/1 oz fresh yeast
2 teaspoons olive oil
1 teaspoon honey
250 ml/8 fl oz tepid water

Put the flour and salt into a mixing bowl. Crumble the yeast into a jug and add the oil, honey and water. Stir until the yeast has dissolved and pour the liquid on to the flour. Mix everything together with your hands to form a dough, turn it out on to a lightly floured surface and knead it for 10 minutes, until smooth. Return it to the bowl, cover and leave the dough in a warm place to double in size.

Divide the dough into six equal pieces (or into three, if you are dealing with half of the dough at a time). Roll each into a ball and flatten this to a 5 mm/$\frac{1}{4}$ in thick oval, using a lightly floured rolling pin. Dust the pitta breads with a little flour, cover and leave them to prove in a warm place for about 20 minutes.

Set the oven at hot (230 C, 450 F, gas 8). After 10 minutes' proving time, put a greased baking tray into the oven and leave it to heat through. When the pitta breads are ready, quickly slide them on to the hot tray and bake them at the top of the oven for 10 minutes. Remove them from the oven and leave them to cool on a wire rack. Each should have risen in the centre to form a pouch. When cold, split the breads open and fill this pouch with salad, soft cheese, savoury spreads or hard-boiled egg for a light lunch dish.

Chapatis

Makes 12

Not really a bread in the sense we know, but these are standard fare in India and are simple to prepare. Serve them with all kinds of curries.

350 g/12 oz wholemeal flour
1 teaspoon sea salt
about 300 ml/½ pint cold water

Sift 275 g/10 oz of the flour into a bowl and sprinkle in the bran from the sieve. Stir in the salt and gradually add the water, mixing everything together to a dough. Knead the dough well for 4 minutes, as this helps to incorporate air. Cover and leave it to stand for at least 1 hour. Knead the dough again and, if it seems a little dry, add a little more water. Divide it into 12, roll each portion into a ball and press flat. Coat the chapatis with the remaining flour.

Heat a lightly greased griddle or heavy-based frying pan until very hot. Place the chapatis, one at a time, on the heated surface, cook one side lightly for about ½ minute and then turn over. Help the chapati to rise during cooking by holding the sides down with two wooden spoons: this traps the air underneath and forces the chapati to rise. Place the chapati under a warmed grill or in a hot oven to keep warm while you cook the remaining ones.

Pizza Pie

Illustrated on pages 60–61

Serves 4

SAUCE
100 g/4 oz onion
2 cloves garlic
1 red pepper
450 g/1 lb fresh or 1 (425-g/15-oz) can tomatoes
2 teaspoons olive oil
1 teaspoon dried oregano
¼ teaspoon marjoram
freshly ground black pepper

BASE
225 g/8 oz wholemeal flour
pinch of sea salt
15 g/½ oz fresh yeast
1 (25-mg) vitamin C tablet, crushed
150 ml/¼ pint tepid water
1 teaspoon olive oil

TOPPING
100 g/4 oz mushrooms
1 green pepper
175 g/6 oz Mozzarella cheese
1 teaspoon dried oregano

GARNISHES (OPTIONAL)
drained canned anchovies and tuna
black olives
sweet corn kernels

Begin by making the sauce so the flavours can develop while you prepare the dough. Finely chop the onion and crush the garlic. Quarter, core and finely chop the red pepper. Cut crosses in the bases of the fresh tomatoes, if used, cover them with boiling water, drain and peel away the skins. Heat the oil in a pan and sauté the onion and garlic together for 4 minutes, without browning them. Add the pepper, fresh or canned tomatoes, the oregano and marjoram to the pan and bring the sauce to the boil. Cover the pan, reduce the heat and simmer for at least 20 minutes while you prepare the dough. Season with black pepper to taste.

Place the flour and salt in a bowl. Crumble the yeast with the crushed vitamin C tablet into a jug and add the tepid water. Stir in the oil. When the yeast has dissolved, pour the mixture on to the flour and, using your hands, bring everything together to form a soft dough. Turn this on to a lightly floured surface and knead it for 5 minutes. Cover with the upturned bowl and leave it to rest for 10 minutes.

While the dough is resting, prepare the topping. Wipe and slice the mushrooms. Quarter, core and chop the green pepper. Finely slice the cheese.

Lightly grease a 20 cm/8 in round flan dish or a large baking sheet. Set the oven at hot (220 C, 425 F, gas 7). Roll the dough out to a 20 cm/8 in round and place it in the flan dish or on the baking sheet. Spread the tomato sauce over the dough to within 1 cm/$\frac{1}{2}$ in of the edge all round and arrange the sliced mushrooms, green pepper and any preferred garnishes on top. Finish with the sliced Mozzarella, sprinkle the pizza with oregano and leave it in a warm place to let the base rise (20–25 minutes). Bake it in the preheated oven for 25–30 minutes, until the base is firm and the cheese is bubbling. Serve at once.

Hot Cross Buns

Illustrated on pages 38–39

Makes 8

225 g/8 oz wholemeal flour
25 g/1 oz soft vegetable margarine
4½ tablespoons tepid skimmed milk
15 g/½ oz fresh yeast
1 (25-mg) vitamin C tablet, crushed
2 teaspoons honey
1 free-range egg, beaten
1 teaspoon mixed spice
pinch of nutmeg
1 tablespoon grated lemon rind
50 g/2 oz currants
50 g/2 oz sultanas
skimmed milk to glaze
pastry trimmings to decorate (optional)
clear honey to finish

Put the flour in a mixing bowl and rub in the margarine. Stir the warm milk, yeast, crushed vitamin C tablet and honey together until the yeast has dissolved. Pour the liquid into the flour mixture with the beaten egg and mix everything together to form a soft dough. Add more flour if the mixture looks like being too sticky. Turn out and knead the dough on a lightly floured surface for 5–8 minutes, until soft and smooth. Cover with the upturned bowl and leave it to rest for about 10 minutes.

Set the oven at hot (220 C, 425 F, gas 5). Pull the dough out until it is 1 cm/½ in thick. Place the spices, lemon rind and dried fruit in the centre, fold over the rest of the dough and knead thoroughly until the ingredients are well distributed throughout. Divide the dough into eight equal pieces, roll each to a ball and place these on lightly greased baking trays. Roll out the pastry trimmings, if used, to an oblong. Cut it into fine strips and arrange two strips on top of each bun to make a cross. Alternatively, simply mark crosses on the buns with a knife. Cover and leave the buns in a warm place to double in size (20–25 minutes). Glaze them with milk and bake them at the top of the oven for 15–20 minutes, until they sound hollow when tapped underneath. Put the buns on wire racks, brush them with honey and leave them to cool.

Top to bottom: Mushroom Soufflé Quiche (page 69), Chicken and Cucumber Flan (page 70), Cod and Courgette Quiche (page 68)

Chelsea Buns

Illustrated on page 27

Makes 8

225 g/8 oz wholemeal flour
40 g/1½ oz unsalted butter or soft vegetable margarine
4½ tablespoons tepid skimmed milk
3 tablespoons tepid water
15 g/½ oz fresh yeast
1 (25-mg) vitamin C tablet, crushed
2 teaspoons clear honey
1 free-range egg, beaten
50 g/2 oz dried apricots, chopped
50 g/2 oz sultanas
25 g/1 oz demerara sugar
¼ teaspoon cinnamon
clear honey to glaze

Sift the flour into a mixing bowl and add the bran left in the sieve. Rub in two thirds of the butter or margarine. Stir the milk, water, yeast, crushed vitamin C tablet and honey together until the yeast has dissolved and pour the mixture on to the flour with the beaten egg. Mix everything together to form a soft dough, adding a little more water if necessary. Turn the dough out on a lightly floured surface and knead it for about 5 minutes, until smooth. Cover with the upturned bowl and leave it to rest for 10 minutes.

Set the oven at hot (230 C, 450 F, gas 8). Melt the remaining butter or margarine. Lightly grease an 18 cm/7 in sandwich tin. Roll the dough out to a 30 × 20 cm/12 × 8 in rectangle, spread it with the melted butter or margarine and sprinkle the chopped apricots, sultanas, sugar and cinnamon on top. Roll the rectangle up from the longest side, cut the roll into eight pieces and arrange these in the greased tin, cut side up, with one in the centre. Cover and leave the buns in a warm place to prove until doubled in size (20–25 minutes). Bake them in the centre of the oven for 15–20 minutes. As soon as they come out, brush them with honey and leave to cool in the tin.

Teacakes

Illustrated on pages 118–119

Makes 6

225 g/8 oz wholemeal flour
25 g/1 oz soft vegetable margarine
4½ tablespoons tepid skimmed milk
15 g/½ oz fresh yeast
1 (25-mg) vitamin C tablet, crushed
2 teaspoons honey
1 free-range egg, beaten
1 teaspoon mixed spice
75 g/3 oz currants
skimmed milk to glaze

Place the flour in a mixing bowl and rub in the margarine. Stir the milk, yeast, crushed vitamin C tablet and honey together until the yeast has dissolved. Pour the mixture on to the flour with the beaten egg and mix everything together to form a soft dough. Add more flour if it looks too sticky. Turn the dough out on to a lightly floured surface and knead it for 5–8 minutes, until soft and smooth. Cover with the upturned bowl and leave it to rest for 10 minutes.

Set the oven at hot (220 C, 425 F, gas 7). Lightly grease two baking trays. Pull the dough out until it is 1 cm/½ in thick and put the mixed spice and currants in the centre. Fold the rest of the dough on top and knead thoroughly for a few minutes. Cut the dough into six equal pieces and roll each to a flat round. Tuck the edges in underneath and shape each piece again to a round (this gives a smoother shape). Arrange the rounds on the greased baking trays, spaced well apart, cover and leave them in a warm place for about 20 minutes, until doubled in size. Glaze the teacakes with milk and bake them at the top of the oven for 15–20 minutes, until each sounds hollow when tapped underneath. Serve as they are, hot or cold, or split them in half and toast them.

Top to bottom: Golden Lentil Pasties (page 66), Fish and Egg Pie (page 74), Curried Root Pie (page 70)

Sultana Swirls

Illustrated on page 30

Makes 8

225 g/8 oz wholemeal flour
½ teaspoon mixed spice
25 g/1 oz soft vegetable margarine
4½ tablespoons tepid skimmed milk
15 g/½ oz fresh yeast
1 (25-mg) vitamin C tablet, crushed
2 teaspoons clear honey
1 free-range egg
100 g/4 oz sultanas
25 g/1 oz hazelnuts, finely chopped
beaten free-range egg to glaze

Put the flour and spice in a bowl and rub in the margarine. Stir the milk, yeast, crushed vitamin C tablet and honey together until the yeast has dissolved. Beat the egg and pour it on to the flour mixture with the yeast liquid. Bring the dough together with your hands until it is soft but not sticky; add more flour if it seems too wet. Turn it on to a lightly floured surface and knead in the sultanas and hazelnuts. Knead for 5 minutes, until smooth and silky. Cover with the upturned bowl and leave the dough to rest for about 10 minutes.

Lightly grease a baking tray and set the oven at hot (220 C, 425 F, gas 7). Divide the rested dough into eight equal pieces. Roll each out to a strip or sausage, about 20 cm/8 in long, tie it into a loose knot and arrange it on the prepared baking tray. Cover and leave the swirls to prove in a warm place until doubled in size (20–25 minutes). Glaze them with beaten egg and bake them at the top of the oven for 12–15 minutes, until they are golden brown and sound hollow when tapped underneath. Place the swirls on a wire rack to cool.

Danish Pastries

Illustrated on page 30

Makes 8

225 g/8 oz wholemeal flour
25 g/1 oz soft vegetable margarine
4½ tablespoons tepid skimmed milk
15 g/½ oz fresh yeast
1 (25-mg) vitamin C tablet, crushed
2 teaspoons clear honey
1 free-range egg, beaten
75 g/3 oz unsalted butter
beaten egg white to glaze

FILLINGS

50 g/2 oz raisins or sultanas
1 small cooking apple, peeled, cored and grated
25 g/1 oz demerara sugar

*

50 g/2 oz ground almonds
1 teaspoon fresh orange juice
1 teaspoon grated orange rind
white of a free-range egg, beaten

*

no-added-sugar jam

Sift the flour into a bowl and add the bran from the sieve. Rub in the margarine. Stir the milk, yeast, crushed vitamin C tablet and honey together until the yeast has dissolved, then pour the mixture on to the flour with the beaten egg. Bring everything together with your hands to form a soft dough; if it is too sticky, add a little extra flour. Turn it on to a lightly floured surface and knead it for 5–8 minutes, until smooth. Cover with the upturned bowl and leave it to rest for 10 minutes.

Divide the butter into four. Return three portions to the refrigerator. Roll the dough out to a 30 × 20 cm/12 × 8 in rectangle with the shortest side nearest to you. Cut the portion of butter into flakes and scatter these over the top two thirds of the dough. Fold the bottom third over the middle and the top third over the bottom, seal the edges and place the dough in the refrigerator to chill for 20 minutes. Repeat this rolling, folding and chilling process three more times, using up the remaining three portions of butter. The dough is now ready to use.

Set the oven at hot (220 C, 425 F, gas 7). Lightly grease a large baking sheet. Decide which fillings you want to use and mix together the appropriate ingredients for each. Take the dough out of the refrigerator and use it to make any of the following shapes:

Pinwheels and Tivolis

Roll the dough out to a 30 × 15 cm/12 × 6 in rectangle and cut this into eight 7.5 cm/3 in squares. Place a spoonful of the chosen filling in the centre of four of the squares, cut from each corner to within 1 cm/½ in of the centre and go round the square, folding alternate points over the filling to make a pinwheel.

For the remaining four squares, arrange a spoonful of a different filling in a strip diagonally across the centre of each, fold the two free corners on top and press together to seal.

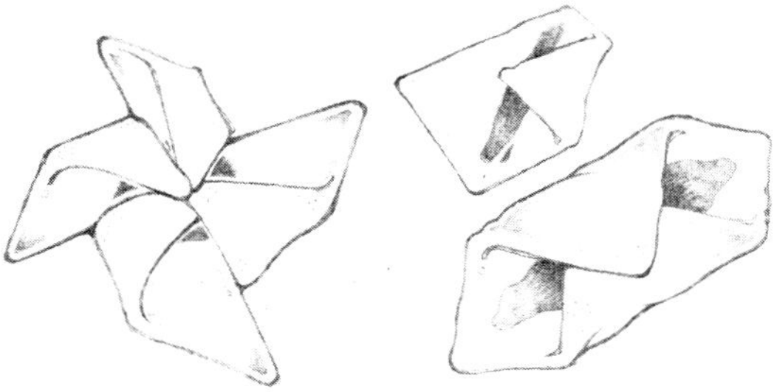

Crescents

Alternatively, roll the dough out to a 25 cm/10 in round, cut it into eight segments and place a little filling at the base of each triangle. Roll up each triangle from the base, sticking the point down firmly, and curve the ends round to form a crescent.

Arrange all the pastries on the baking sheet and leave them to prove in a warm place until doubled in size (20–25 minutes). Glaze them with beaten egg white and bake them in the preheated oven for 15–20 minutes

Swedish Tea Ring

Illustrated on page 27

225 g/8 oz wholemeal flour
25 g/1 oz soft vegetable margarine
4½ tablespoons tepid skimmed milk
15 g/½ oz fresh yeast
1 (25-mg) vitamin C tablet, crushed
2 teaspoons clear honey · 1 free-range egg, beaten

FILLING

25 g/1 oz soft vegetable margarine, melted
100 g/4 oz raisins
50 g/2 oz walnuts, finely chopped
grated rind of half an orange
1 teaspoon cinnamon

GLAZE

beaten egg white · clear honey

Sift the flour into a bowl and add the bran left in the sieve. Rub in the margarine until the mixture resembles fine breadcrumbs. Stir the milk, yeast, vitamin C and honey together until the yeast has dissolved, then pour the mixture on to the flour and add the beaten egg. Using your hands, bring the dough together, adding more flour if the mixture is too sticky. Turn it out on to a lightly floured surface and knead the dough for 5–8 minutes. Cover with the upturned bowl and leave it to rest for 10 minutes.

Set the oven at hot (220 C, 425 F, gas 7) and lightly grease a baking tray. Roll the dough out to a 40 × 18 cm/16 × 7 in rectangle. Spread this with the melted margarine and sprinkle the raisins, walnuts, orange rind and cinnamon on top. Starting from the long side, roll the dough up like a swiss roll. Arrange the roll in a circle on the baking tray, joining the ends so that it forms a complete ring. Make cuts around the ring at 2.5 cm/1 in intervals and spread one side of each cut open so that a ripple runs round the ring in one direction. Cover and leave it to rise in a warm place. Glaze it with egg white and bake it in the centre of the oven for 20–25 minutes, until it is golden brown and sounds hollow when tapped underneath. Lift the ring on to a wire cooling rack and brush it with honey.

Bara Brith

Illustrated on pages 38–39

Makes one 450 g/1 lb loaf

A traditional Welsh bread, full of fruit and spices.

225 g/8 oz wholemeal flour
50 g/2 oz soft vegetable margarine
1 teaspoon mixed spice
¼ teaspoon nutmeg
50 g/2 oz raisins
50 g/2 oz sultanas
40 g/1½ oz currants
grated rind of a lemon
4½ tablespoons tepid skimmed milk
3 tablespoons tepid water
15 g/½ oz fresh yeast
1 teaspoon clear honey
1 small free-range egg, beaten
1 teaspoon clear honey mixed with 1 teaspoon boiling water to glaze

Sift the flour into a bowl and rub in the margarine until the mixture resembles fine breadcrumbs. Add the spices, dried fruit and grated lemon rind. Stir the milk, water, yeast and honey together until the yeast has dissolved, then pour the liquid on to the dry ingredients with half the beaten egg, and knead everything together to form a dough. Turn out on to a lightly floured surface and knead the dough for 5 minutes, until soft and smooth. Put it back in the bowl, cover it with a damp cloth and leave it in a warm place until it has doubled in size (this will take 1–1¼ hours).

Set the oven at hot (230 C, 450 F, gas 8). Knead the dough again and place it in a greased 450 g/1 lb loaf tin. Cover it with a cloth and leave it in a warm place to double in size once more. Glaze the top with the remaining beaten egg and bake the loaf for 20–25 minutes, until it sounds hollow when tipped out of its tin and tapped underneath. Complete the glaze by brushing the top of the loaf with a little honey mixture, leave it to cool and serve it sliced and buttered.

Christmas Stollen

This wholefood version omits the conventional candied fruits and uses fresh lemon rind instead.

225 g/8 oz wholemeal flour
25 g/1 oz soft vegetable margarine
4½ tablespoons tepid skimmed milk
15 g/½ oz fresh yeast
1 (25-mg) vitamin C tablet, crushed
2 teaspoons clear honey
1 free-range egg, beaten
100 g/4 oz raisins
50 g/2 oz finely chopped almonds
grated rind of a lemon
skimmed milk or beaten egg white to glaze
1 teaspoon honey mixed with 1 teaspoon boiling water to glaze

Put the flour in a bowl and rub in the margarine. Stir the milk, yeast, crushed vitamin C tablet and honey together until the yeast has dissolved. Pour the liquid on to the flour mixture with the beaten egg. Using your hands, bring the mixture together to form a soft but not sticky dough. Turn on to a lightly floured surface and knead it for 5–8 minutes, until smooth and silky. Cover with the upturned bowl and leave the dough to rest for 10 minutes.

Set the oven at moderately hot (200 C, 400 F, gas 6) and lightly grease a baking tray. Gently pull the rested dough into an oblong and place the raisins, almonds and lemon rind on top. Fold the rest of the dough on top and knead thoroughly to mix in the fruit and nuts. Gently roll the dough out to an oval, a generous 5 mm/¼ in thick. Fold the oval almost in half lengthways, so that the top edge comes to within 1 cm/½ in of the lower edge, place it on the baking tray and press to seal the edges. Cover and leave the Stollen in a warm place to double in size. Brush it with milk or beaten egg white and bake it in the centre of the oven for 25–30 minutes, until it sounds hollow when tapped underneath. Transfer the Stollen to a wire rack and brush it with honey glaze. Leave it to cool and serve it sliced.

QUICK BREADS

Breads, both sweet and savoury, can be made without yeast. These are known as quick breads because the raising agents used work more quickly than yeast, so preparation time is reduced. They are made rather like scones and have a different texture from yeast breads. Most popular of this type of bread are the teabreads made with dried fruits and spices which are sliced and buttered. Corn bread, Irish soda breads and other savoury loaves are useful standbys when yeast isn't available, time is limited and a bread is required.

Irish Soda Bread

Illustrated on page 23

Makes one large loaf

450 g / 1 lb wholemeal flour
$2\frac{1}{2}$ teaspoons baking powder
$\frac{1}{2}$ teaspoon salt
300 ml / $\frac{1}{2}$ pint buttermilk
about 150 ml / $\frac{1}{4}$ pint skimmed milk

Set the oven at hot (220 C, 425 F, gas 7). Lightly grease a baking tray. Sift the flour, baking powder and salt into a mixing bowl and add the bran remaining in the sieve. Stir in the buttermilk with a round-bladed knife and add just enough skimmed milk to mix the ingredients to a soft dough. Turn out on to a work surface and knead the dough gently, forming it into a 20 cm / 8 in round. Place the bread on the baking tray and cut a large cross through the centre, from top to bottom and from side to side. Glaze the loaf with any remaining skimmed milk and bake it in the centre of the oven for 25–30 minutes, until well risen and golden brown. Break it into the four segments made by the cross, if liked, and serve it hot, sliced and buttered.

Cornbread

Illustrated on page 23

Cuts into 12 pieces

175 g / 6 oz cornmeal
75 g / 3 oz wholemeal flour
2 teaspoons baking powder
pinch of sea salt
50 g / 2 oz soft vegetable margarine
1 free-range egg
250 ml / 8 fl oz skimmed milk

Preheat the oven to moderately hot (200 C, 400 F, gas 6). Lightly grease a shallow 20 cm / 8 in square tin. Mix the cornmeal, wholemeal flour, baking powder and salt together in a bowl and rub in the margarine until the mixture resembles fine breadcrumbs. Beat the egg with the milk and stir the liquid into the flour mixture. When thoroughly combined, pour the dough into the prepared tin and bake it in the centre of the oven for 25 to 30 minutes, until firm to the touch. Serve it at once, cut into fingers.

Cornbread can be served with savoury or sweet dishes but it does not keep well.

Spiced Honey Bread

Illustrated on page 27

Makes one 450 g/1 lb loaf

225 g/8 oz wholemeal flour
2 teaspoons baking powder
½ teaspoon cinnamon
½ teaspoon ground ginger
5 tablespoons clear honey
1 free-range egg
200 ml/7 fl oz skimmed milk

Set the oven at moderate (180 C, 350 F, gas 4). Lightly grease a 450 g/1 lb loaf tin. Sift the flour, baking powder and spices into a mixing bowl. Add the honey, egg and milk and, using an electric mixer, beat all the ingredients together for 5 minutes. Spoon the dough into the tin, level the top and bake it in the centre of the oven for 25–30 minutes. Take the honey bread out of the tin and serve it sliced, either warm or cold.

Banana and Hazelnut Bread

Illustrated on pages 38–39

Makes one 450 g/1 lb loaf

225 g/8 oz wholemeal flour
1½ teaspoons baking powder
40 g/1½ oz chopped hazelnuts
1 large banana
1 free-range egg
2 tablespoons skimmed milk
50 g/2 oz soft vegetable margarine
1 tablespoon clear honey

Set the oven at moderate (180 C, 350 F, gas 4). Lightly grease a 450 g/1 lb loaf tin. Sift the flour and baking powder into a bowl and add the bran remaining in the sieve. Stir in the chopped hazelnuts. Mash the banana in a separate bowl and beat in the egg. Beat the two together until smooth, then add the milk. Melt the margarine with the honey over a low heat. Add the banana mixture and the melted margarine to the dry ingredients and mix them in thoroughly. Turn the dough into the tin, smooth the top and bake it in the centre of the oven for 20–25 minutes, until firm to the touch. Leave the bread to cool in the tin.

Malt Loaf

Illustrated on page 27

Makes one 450 g/1 lb loaf

225 g/8 oz wholemeal flour
2 teaspoons baking powder
75 g/3 oz dates, chopped
3 tablespoons malt extract
2 tablespoons clear honey
150 ml/¼ pint skimmed milk
1 free-range egg

Preheat the oven to moderately hot (200 C, 400 F, gas 6). Grease a 450 g/1 lb loaf tin. Sift the flour and baking powder into a bowl. Add the chopped dates. Gently heat the malt extract, honey and milk in a pan together until the malt and honey have dissolved, pour the mixture on to the dry ingredients and add the egg. Beat everything together thoroughly, transfer the dough to the tin and bake it in the centre of the oven for 30–40 minutes, until firm, reducing the heat slightly towards the end of the cooking time if the loaf looks like browning too much. Tip the loaf out of its tin and leave it to cool. Serve it sliced and buttered.

The key to perfect pastry is lightness. Shortcrust, rough puff, flaky or choux, whatever the name, the aim remains the same – to incorporate air. Many people are reluctant to try making pastry with wholemeal flour. The idea that a coarse flour could be transformed into a light pastry seems unbelievable, but follow the guidelines in this chapter and you will find success.

Admittedly, it is hard to achieve the fine, light layers characteristic of puff pastry, but the high level of fat required for this makes it rather unsuitable for a healthy diet anyway. Instead, flaky and rough puff pastries are both easier to make and perfectly suitable for special occasions. Again, their high level of fat rules out an everyday role for them, but for occasional use in pies and plaits where extra fine pastry is required, wholemeal versions of these two conventional recipes work well.

It is shortcrust pastry, containing a lower level of fat, that is ideal for everyday use. It is also versatile, as it can be given different flavours for different uses. Extra care is needed in making shortcrust pastry with wholemeal flour; heavy hands, overkneading and too little water all help to make a pastry hard and dull. More than with white flour, it is essential to respect the basic guidelines for making perfect pastry: keep everything cool, handle the pastry as little as possible and stick to the right proportions of fat, flour and water. You will find that this extra effort really pays off when you produce a pastry with a nutty richness of flavour and texture that leaves white pastry completely in the shade.

Top to bottom: Prawn Puffs (page 76), Ratatouille Puff (page 75), Savoury Spinach Choux (page 77)

Shortcrust Pastry

Makes 100 g/4 oz

100 g/4 oz wholemeal flour
pinch of sea salt (optional)
50 g/2 oz soft vegetable margarine
cold water to mix

Sift the flour into a mixing bowl and add the bran remaining in the sieve. If you are using salt, stir it into the flour.

Cut the margarine into small pieces and rub them into the flour, using your fingertips. As you do so, lift your hands up from the bowl so that

air becomes trapped as the mixture falls back into the bowl. Continue rubbing in the fat in this way until the mixture resembles fine breadcrumbs. If you have time, chill this rubbed-in mixture in the refrigerator for at least 15 minutes, as the fat and flour seem to absorb water more readily and evenly when cold. You could use this time to prepare your pie or pastry filling, if you like.

Sprinkle 4 teaspoons cold water over the flour mixture and mix it in, using a round-bladed knife to cut through the flour. This helps to incorporate the water without raising the temperature of the ingredients with the warmth of your hand. When the flour has started to clump together, finish off by gently kneading the mixture to form a dough: if it will not combine, add a little more water. Chill the pastry in the refrigerator until you want to use it.

Dust a worktop or pastry board with a little flour and dust your rolling pin, too, to stop the pastry sticking. Roll the pastry away from you, lightly and evenly, with short strokes. Bear in mind the shape you want your pastry to be: circular for a flan, rectangular for a slice and so on. When you want to roll the pastry in a different direction, turn it around on your worktop and continue rolling away from you; never roll from side to side. Take care not to roll the pastry too thin: it should be around 3 mm/⅛ in thick. Don't stretch the pastry to fit your dish; you will find that it shrinks on cooking. Treat your pastry lightly – and you will be rewarded with a light result. If you are heavyhanded, then your pastry will be hard, tough and dry.

Variations

Cheese Pastry

Add a pinch of mustard powder, cayenne or paprika to the flour and rub in the fat as directed. Mix in 50 g/2 oz finely grated cheese, followed by an egg yolk and just enough cold water to bind the pastry together. This will give you a rich, savoury pastry with added protein.

Oat Pastry

Make the pastry as directed but use 115 g/4½ oz wholemeal flour mixed with 50 g/2 oz rolled oats and rub in 75 g/3 oz margarine. Rolled oats give pastry a nice, hearty texture as well as extra fibre.

Sesame Pastry

Mix 1 tablespoon sesame seeds into the flour for extra protein and flavour.

Granary Pastry

Replace half the wholemeal flour with Granary flour for a crunchy pastry, good for pasties and vegetable pies.

Sweet Pastry

You do not need to add sugar to pastry which is to be used for sweet fillings; these will be sweet enough in themselves. Simply use an egg yolk to help bind the ingredients together; this will give the pastry extra flavour.

Flaky Pastry

Makes 225 g/8 oz

225 g/8 oz wholemeal flour
pinch of sea salt (optional)
175 g/6 oz unsalted butter or block margarine
2 teaspoons lemon juice
6–8 tablespoons cold water

Sift the flour into a mixing bowl and add the bran left in the sieve. Stir in the salt, if used. Divide the fat into four portions. Place three in the refrigerator and cut the fourth into small pieces. Rub them thoroughly into the flour, as for Shortcrust Pastry (see opposite).

Sprinkle on the lemon juice and 6 tablespoons cold water. Mix with a round-bladed knife and bring the dough together with your hands, adding more water, until it is soft but not sticky.

Turn out on to a lightly floured surface and knead thoroughly until the dough is soft and silky. Shape it roughly into an oblong, then roll it into a 38 × 13 cm/15 × 5 in rectangle, with the shortest sides facing you. Brush off any surplus flour.

Divide another portion of fat into small pieces. Dot these across the top two thirds of the dough. Fold the bottom third over the middle and the top third over the bottom and seal the edges. Put the dough on a plate, cover and leave it

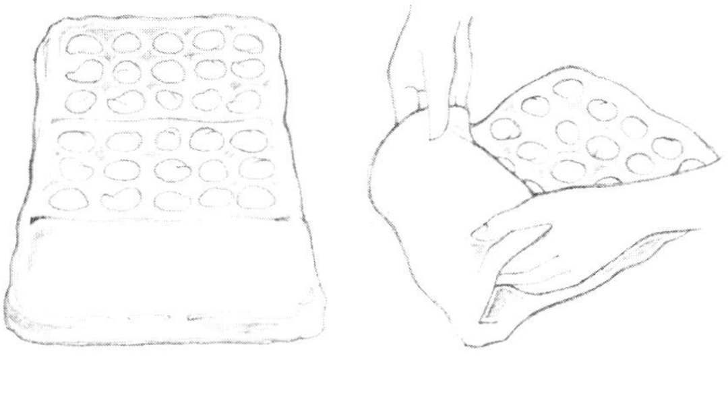

to rest in the refrigerator for 20 minutes. Repeat the rolling, folding and chilling process twice more, using up the remaining two portions of fat. Roll the dough out to a rectangle for the last time, fold this into three and return it to the refrigerator to rest for 20 minutes.

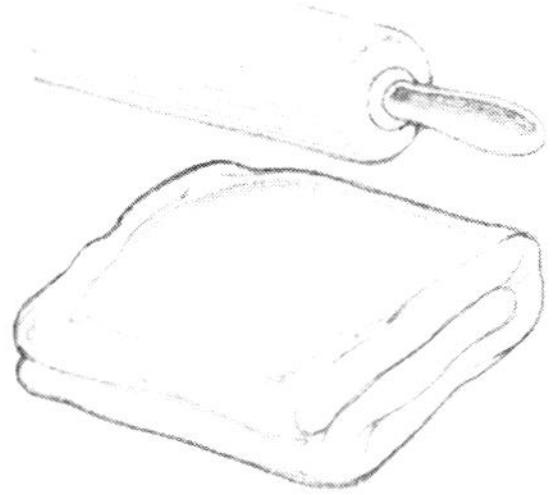

Your pastry is now ready. Roll it out 5 mm/$\frac{1}{4}$ in thick, or as required. Alternatively, you can freeze it, wrapped in greaseproof paper and sealed in a thick polythene bag. Thaw for 3–4 hours before use.

Rough Puff Pastry

Rough puff is made in a similar way to flaky pastry and produces much the same results, but the method is quicker.

Use the same ingredients as for Flaky Pastry, but instead of dividing the fat into four portions, rub it all in at the beginning. Proceed as for Flaky Pastry, rolling, folding and chilling the dough as instructed. One important difference between the two pastries is that the dough for rough puff must not be kneaded prior to rolling out, whereas this is crucial to the success of flaky pastry.

OVERLEAF *clockwise, from left*: Pizza Pie (page 44), Oaty Leek Pie (page 71), Tuna and Sweet Corn Quiche (page 68), Sponge Fruit Flan (page 82), Cheese and Mushroom Plait (page 40)

USING PASTRY

Flans

Sweet and savoury flans may be cooked in either metal or ceramic flan dishes or in metal rings placed on flat baking trays. Whichever utensil is used, care is needed in rolling out the pastry to fit the flan dish without stretching. Stretched pastry will just return and shrink during cooking, giving unsightly uneven edges to the flan. To avoid this, roll the pastry out to a round about 1 cm/$\frac{1}{2}$ in larger all round than the dish. Lift the pastry by folding it gently down over the rolling pin and lower it over the flan dish. Gently fit the pastry into the dish, pressing down to make a firm 'seam' around the inside edge. If the dish has fluted edges, gently ease the pastry into the flutes so that the baked case will be even. Finish by rolling the rolling pin across the top of the dish to cut off any excess pastry.

Some recipes call for a baked flan case. This is achieved by baking the pastry 'blind', without the filling. This is obviously necessary if the filling itself is not to be cooked, but some quiches also benefit from being made in flan cases that have already been baked blind, as this prevents the pastry from becoming soggy. It is also useful to keep a number of cooked, empty flan cases in your freezer.

To bake blind, fit a sheet of greaseproof paper over the pastry flan case to protect the base and sides from drying out too much, and anchor it by scattering dried beans or pasta on top (these will also prevent the pastry base from rising up during baking). Bake the flan in a moderately hot oven (200 C, 400 F, gas 6) for 10 minutes. Remove the paper and, if the flan isn't to be cooked further with the filling, return it to the oven for a further 5 minutes, until the pastry is cooked through. Do not do this if you are making a quiche, for instance, and the filled flan has to be baked once more, or the pastry may then become too dry.

Open Tarts

Tarts are traditionally filled with a jam, marmalade or mincemeat filling, decorated perhaps with lattice work strips of pastry and baked on shallow pie plates. For healthier varieties of jam, use those made without added sugar. Whole Earth and Country Basket ranges are sweetened with fruit juices and have a much higher level of fruit than conventional jams.

To make a tart, roll out the pastry (Sweet Shortcrust, page 58, is suitable) to a round 2.5 cm/1 in larger than the plate. Fold the round over the rolling pin and lower it over the plate. Smooth the pastry down into the centre of the dish and around the sides and trim off the excess by running a knife around the edge of the plate. Roll out these trimmings, cut them into long strips and arrange these over the filled tart in a lattice pattern. Glaze the pastry with milk.

Single Crust Pies

These are pies which simply have a topping of pastry, baked either in deep pie dishes or on shallow pie plates.

Put the filling inside the dish. Roll the pastry out to fit on top of the dish, allowing an extra $1\,\mathrm{cm}/\frac{1}{2}\,\mathrm{in}$ all round. Cut a fine strip of pastry from your pastry shape to fit the rim of the dish, position it on the rim and brush it with a little cold water. Fold the main piece of pastry over your rolling pin and lower it on to the dish. Cut off any surplus with a knife and seal the edges all round by pressing lightly with your fingers.

Now knock up the edge with the back of a knife (1); this helps the pastry to open out into layers and gives an attractive finish. Simply strike the pastry in several places at each point all the way round.

1

Flute the edges, beginning at the far side of the dish (2). Press the top of the pastry with the thumb and, using the back of a knife, draw the edge towards the centre for about $1\,\mathrm{cm}/\frac{1}{2}\,\mathrm{in}$. Continue all the way round the pastry edge. Alternatively, you can simply crimp the edge by pinching a piece between the thumb and forefinger of both hands and twisting in opposite directions (3). Continue this all the way round the edge of the pie.

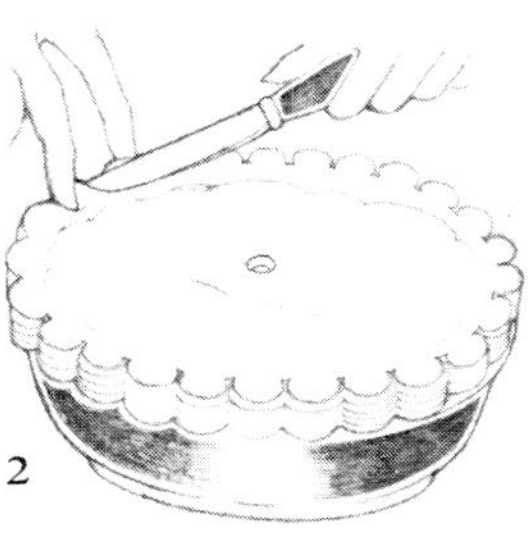

2

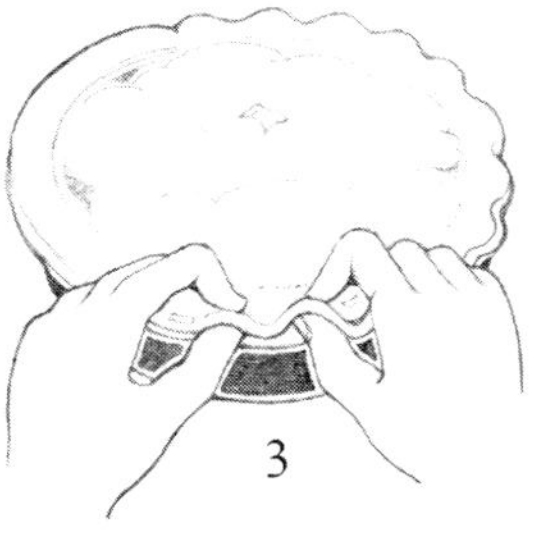

3

If you prefer, you can fork the pie edges by pressing the back of a fork all the way round, with the prongs facing the centre (4).

Finally, make a small hole in the top of the pie to let steam escape and decorate it, if liked, with pastry leaves (5). Roll out any pastry trimmings and cut them into $2.5\,\mathrm{cm}/1$ in-wide strips. Cut these diagonally into diamond shapes and mark veins on them with a knife. Pinch one end of each and arrange the leaves around the steam hole.

Finish by glazing the top of the pie with milk.

4

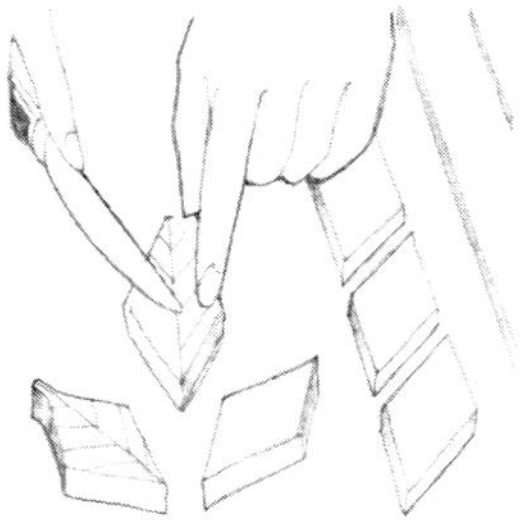

5

Double Crust Pies

A double crust pie is made in much the same way as a single crust pie, but with a layer of pastry both above and below the filling.

Roll out half the pastry to line the base and sides of the dish, ease it inside and trim the edges with a knife. Roll out the remaining half of pastry to make a lid, as for Single Crust Pies (above). Put the filling in the pie and moisten the pastry rim with a little cold water. Lift the lid on to the dish, trim away the surplus pastry and press down to seal the edges together. Knock up and flute the edges as for Single Crust Pies (above), make steam outlets in the surface and glaze the top, ready for baking.

Choux Pastry

Choux pastry is quite different from the other pastries described here, but the basic aim of incorporating air for a light, well-risen pastry remains the same. In many ways it is simpler to use than other pastries: there is no rolling out, as the pastry is either spooned or piped on to baking trays, ready for baking in a hot oven.

Choux pastry is the perfect answer to special occasions; éclairs and profiteroles form impressive and tempting desserts (and can contain all sorts of fillings, not just rich cream), while savoury choux pastry makes for original starters and main courses. Unfortunately, this is the only pastry for which wholemeal flour does not give good results; 81 or 85 per cent wheatmeal flours work much better.

50 g/2 oz soft vegetable margarine
150 ml/¼ pint cold water
65 g/2½ oz 81 or 85 per cent wheatmeal flour, sifted
2 free-range eggs

Set the oven at hot (220 C, 425 F, gas 7). Place the margarine and water in a pan and heat until the margarine has melted. Bring the mixture to the boil and quickly pour in the sifted flour. Beat it in immediately, take the pan off the heat and continue beating the mixture until it is smooth, glossy and comes away from the side of the pan.

Add one egg and beat it in thoroughly until no traces remain. Add the second egg and again beat it in thoroughly.

The mixture is now ready to use. Place dessertspoonfuls of it on to lightly greased baking trays, spaced well apart, for profiteroles, or to make éclairs, pipe it on to the trays in 5 cm/2 in or 7.5 cm/3 in lengths, using a large, plain nozzle. Bake the choux in the preheated oven for 15 minutes. Turn the oven down to moderately hot (190 C, 375 F, gas 5) to finish cooking (10–15 minutes). Test to see if the choux pastry is done by lightly pressing the sides of the éclairs or profiteroles. If the sides 'give' under the pressure, the pastry needs a few minutes longer. If they are firm to the touch, it is ready. Remove the choux from the oven and slit the sides along the base to let the steam escape. Return them to the oven for a further 5 minutes to dry out. Cool them on a wire rack before filling.

Traditionally, éclairs and profiteroles are filled with whipped double cream. You can lower the fat content of the filling by using whipping cream instead, or even better, low fat soft cheese mixed with a little chopped fresh fruit. Melted carob makes a healthier coating than chocolate and still gives a rich, chocolate-like taste.

Top to bottom: Franzipan (page 79), Orange Coconut Tart (page 83), Orange and Raisin Cheesecake (page 78), Almond Slice (page 81)

Winter Vegetable Pasties

Illustrated on title page

Makes 5

450 g/1 lb mixed root vegetables (carrot, swede, parsnip, potato, turnip)
50 g/2 oz onion
2 tablespoons vegetable stock
½ teaspoon dried thyme
freshly ground black pepper
350 g/12 oz Cheese Pastry (page 58)
skimmed milk to glaze

Preheat the oven to moderately hot (200 C, 400 F, gas 6). Peel and dice the root vegetables and finely chop the onion. Mix them together with the stock and thyme and season with black pepper.

Divide the cheese pastry into five equal portions and roll each out to an 18 cm/7 in round (use an 18 cm/7 in side plate as a guide). Arrange some filling down the centre of each pastry round. Brush the edge of the circles with a little cold water and bring the two sides up to meet above the filling. Seal the edges together and flute the seam with the back of a knife (see page 63). Transfer the pasties to a baking tray and glaze them with milk. Bake them in the centre of the oven for 15 minutes, then reduce the heat to 190 C, 375 F, gas 5) and continue cooking until the filling is just tender (5–10 minutes) – test this with a skewer or the blade of a small knife. Serve hot or cold.

Golden Lentil Pasties

Illustrated on page 49

Makes 2

50 g/2 oz onion
1 tablespoon oil
½ teaspoon ground cumin
½ teaspoon ground coriander
¼ teaspoon turmeric
½ teaspoon cumin seeds
100 g/4 oz carrots, finely grated
75 g/3 oz split red lentils
300 ml/½ pint cold water
freshly ground black pepper
100 g/4 oz Shortcrust Pastry (page 58)
skimmed milk to glaze

Preheat the oven to moderately hot (200 C, 400 F, gas 6). Finely chop the onion. Sauté it in the oil for a few minutes, without browning. Stir in the spices and cook for 1 minute. Add the grated carrot and the lentils to the pan and mix in well. Pour in the water, bring to the boil, reduce the heat and simmer the mixture for 20 minutes, until the lentils are just soft. Season with black pepper.

Divide the pastry in two and roll each half to an 18 cm/7 in round, using an 18 cm/7 in side plate as a guide. Arrange half the filling down the centre of each round, dampen the pastry edges and bring them up to meet above the filling. Press together to seal and flute the seam with a knife (see page 63). Place the pasties on a baking tray. Glaze them with milk and bake them in the centre of the oven for 20 minutes, until the pastry is golden brown. Serve hot or cold.

Picnic Pasties

Illustrated on pages 72–73

Makes 4

50 g/2 oz onion
4 tablespoons frozen sweet corn kernels, thawed
50 g/2 oz button mushrooms
75 g/3 oz courgettes
50 g/2 oz Cotswold or Cheshire cheese, finely grated
1 tablespoon water
freshly ground black pepper
225 g/8 oz Shortcrust Pastry (page 58)
skimmed milk to glaze

Preheat the oven to moderately hot (200 C, 400 F, gas 6). Finely chop the onion and mix it with the sweet corn in a bowl. Wipe and finely chop the button mushrooms, dice the courgettes and add them to the bowl with the grated cheese, the water and a sprinkling of pepper. Mix everything well together.

Divide the pastry into four and roll each portion out to a 15 cm/6 in round, using a 15 cm/6 in side plate as a guide. Brush the edges of the pastry with cold water and arrange a quarter of the filling down the centre of each round. Bring the pastry edges to meet over the filling, seal them together and flute the seam with the back of a knife (see page 63). Put the pasties on baking trays, glaze them with milk and bake them for 20–25 minutes, until the filling is just soft and the pastry well browned. Serve them hot or cold.

Savoury Nutmeat Rolls

Illustrated on pages 104–105

Makes 16

225 g/8 oz Shortcrust Pastry (page 58)
50 g/2 oz onion
50 g/2 oz carrots
50 g/2 oz mushrooms
2 teaspoons oil
2 tablespoons fresh parsley
pinch of dried thyme
100 g/4 oz fresh wholemeal breadcrumbs
50 g/2 oz ground hazelnuts
50 g/2 oz ground walnuts
1 free-range egg, beaten
2 tablespoons vegetable stock
freshly ground black pepper
milk to glaze

Place the pastry in the refrigerator to chill while you prepare the filling.

Set the oven at moderately hot (200 C, 400 F, gas 6). Finely chop the onion, finely grate the carrots, wipe and chop the mushrooms and sauté the vegetables together in the oil for a few minutes. Take the pan off the heat and stir in the parsley, thyme, breadcrumbs and ground nuts. Bind the mixture with the beaten egg and the stock and season it with black pepper.

Roll the pastry out to a 35 × 25 cm/14 × 10 in rectangle and cut it in half lengthways. Divide the nutmeat filling in two and roll each portion to a long sausage shape. Arrange the sausages on the pastry strips, brush the edges of the pastry with cold water and fold them over the filling to seal. Flute the seams (see page 63) and cut each pastry roll into eight pieces. Put these on baking trays, glaze them with milk and cut little vents in the tops to let steam out. Bake the nutmeat rolls for 20–25 minutes, until golden.

Cod and Courgette Quiche

Illustrated on page 46

Serves 4

100 g/4 oz Shortcrust Pastry (page 58)
225 g/8 oz smoked cod
100 g/4 oz courgettes
50 g/2 oz onion
1 teaspoon oil
2 free-range eggs
150 ml/¼ pint natural yogurt
freshly ground black pepper

Roll the pastry out on a lightly floured surface and use it to line an 18 cm/7 in flan dish. Bake blind (see page 62) in a moderately hot oven (200 C, 400 F, gas 6) for 10 minutes.

Poach the fish in a little water for 8–10 minutes, until just cooked, drain and flake it. Finely slice the courgettes and steam them for 4 minutes. Chop the onion and soften it in the oil for 2 minutes. Combine the onion, courgettes and flaked fish in the cooked pastry case. Beat the eggs and yogurt together, season with pepper and pour the mixture over the filling. Bake the quiche for 25–30 minutes, until firm to the touch. Serve hot or cold.

Leek Quiche

Serves 4

100 g/4 oz Shortcrust Pastry (page 58)
350 g/12 oz leeks
2 free-range eggs
150 ml/¼ pint natural yogurt
sprig of fresh rosemary, chopped, or a pinch of dried rosemary
freshly ground black pepper
50 g/2 oz Cheshire cheese, grated

Roll the pastry out on a lightly floured surface to fit an 18 cm/7 in flan dish. Bake the flan blind (see page 62) in a moderately hot oven (200 C, 400 F, gas 6) for 10 minutes.

Trim the leeks and cut them into 1 cm/½ in rings. Wash them thoroughly, plunge them into boiling water and cook them for 5–7 minutes, until just tender. Drain well and arrange the leeks in the cooked pastry case. Beat the eggs with the yogurt and rosemary. Season with pepper and pour the mixture over the leeks. Top the quiche with grated cheese and bake it in the centre of the oven for 25–30 minutes, until golden brown and set. Serve hot or cold.

Tuna and Sweet Corn Quiche

Illustrated on pages 60–61

Serves 6

175 g/6 oz Shortcrust Pastry (page 58)
100 g/4 oz onion
2 teaspoons oil
1 green pepper
1 (198-g/7-oz) can tuna in brine
4 tablespoons drained canned sweet corn kernels
2 free-range eggs
150 ml/¼ pint natural yogurt
½ teaspoon oregano
freshly ground black pepper
50 g/2 oz Cheddar cheese, grated

Roll the pastry out on a lightly floured surface and use it to line a 20 cm/8 in flan dish. Bake the flan blind (see page 62) in a moderately hot oven (200 C, 400 F, gas 6) for 10 minutes.

While the flan is cooking, prepare the filling. Finely chop the onion and sauté it gently in the oil for a few minutes. Deseed and chop the pepper. Drain the tuna and flake it with a fork. Mix the onion, pepper and tuna together, transfer the mixture to the cooked pastry case and sprinkle the sweet corn on top. Beat together the eggs, yogurt, oregano and pepper and pour the liquid over the filling. Top the quiche with the grated cheese and bake it in the centre of the oven for 25–30 minutes, until golden brown and firm to the touch. Serve hot or cold.

Mushroom Soufflé Quiche

Illustrated on page 46

Serves 4

100 g/4 oz Shortcrust Pastry (page 58)
175 g/6 oz button mushrooms
40 g/1½ oz soft vegetable margarine
15 g/½ oz wholemeal flour
150 ml/¼ pint skimmed milk
2 free-range eggs, separated
pinch of dried thyme
freshly ground black pepper

Roll the pastry out on a lightly floured surface and use it to line an 18 cm/7 in flan ring or dish. Bake the flan blind (see page 62) in a moderately hot oven (200 C, 400 F, gas 6) for 10 minutes; remove the greaseproof paper and bake it for a further 5 minutes.

Wipe the mushrooms and chop them finely. Sauté them in 25 g/1 oz of the margarine until the juices run, then set aside. Melt the remaining margarine in a clean pan and stir in the flour. Cook for 1 minute, then gradually add the milk. Bring to the boil and simmer for 1 minute, stirring constantly. Quickly pour the sauce on to the egg yolks and beat well. Stir in the mushrooms, thyme and pepper. Whisk the egg whites until stiff and fold them into the mixture with a metal spoon. Pour the filling into the flan case and bake the quiche in the centre of the oven for 20–25 minutes. Serve hot.

Aduki Quiche

Serves 4

50 g/2 oz aduki beans, soaked in water overnight
100 g/4 oz wholemeal flour
3 tablespoons oil
3–4 tablespoons cold water
75 g/3 oz onion
½ green pepper, deseeded and chopped
2 free-range eggs
150 ml/¼ pint skimmed milk
½ teaspoon dried thyme
freshly ground black pepper
25 g/1 oz farmhouse Cheddar cheese, grated

Drain the beans, place them in a saucepan and cover them with water. Bring to the boil, lower the heat and simmer them for 1–1½ hours, until just soft.

Sift the flour into a bowl and add the bran left in the sieve. Sprinkle 2 tablespoons of the oil over the flour, followed by 3 tablespoons of the water. Using a round-bladed knife, work in the fluid. Draw the dough together with your fingers; if it feels very dry, add a little more water. Gently knead the dough on a worktop for a few minutes, until silky, wrap it in clingfilm and chill it for 20 minutes.

Set the oven at moderately hot (200 C, 400 F, gas 6). Roll out the rested dough and use it to line an 18 cm/7 in flan ring or dish. Bake the flan blind (see page 62) for 10 minutes. Finely chop the onion and cook it in the remaining oil for a few minutes, without browning. Take the pan off the heat and stir in the chopped green pepper. Drain the cooked aduki beans, add them to the mixture and spread the filling inside the baked pastry case. Beat the eggs with the milk, thyme and pepper and pour the liquid over the filling. Sprinkle the quiche with grated cheese and bake it for 25–30 minutes, until the filling is golden brown and set.

Curried Root Pie

Illustrated on page 49

Serves 2

100 g/4 oz wholemeal flour
50 g/2 oz soft vegetable margarine
1 tablespoon sesame seeds
cold water to mix
FILLING
50 g/2 oz onion
1 tablespoon oil
100 g/4 oz carrot, diced
175 g/6 oz swede, diced
100 g/4 oz parsnip, diced
½ teaspoon ground cumin
½ teaspoon ground coriander
¼ teaspoon turmeric
pinch of cayenne
1 tablespoon wholemeal flour
150 ml/¼ pint vegetable stock
sea salt
freshly ground black pepper
skimmed milk to glaze

Sift the flour into a bowl and add the bran remaining in the sieve. Rub in the margarine until the mixture resembles fine breadcrumbs. Stir in the sesame seeds. Place the mixture in the refrigerator to chill until the filling is ready.

Set the oven at moderately hot (200 C, 400 F, gas 6). Finely chop the onion and sauté it in the oil for 2 minutes. Stir in the diced carrot, swede and parsnip and cook for 1 minute. Mix in the spices. Add the flour and stir it well into all the vegetables. Gradually mix in the vegetable stock, bring the mixture to the boil, cover, reduce the heat and simmer it for 15 minutes.

Add just enough cold water to the flour mixture to make a soft dough. Roll the dough out on a lightly floured surface to a piece 1 cm/½ in larger all round than the top of a deep ovenproof pie dish. Place the filling in the dish and cut a fine strip of pastry from the rolled-out piece to fit round the rim of the dish. Put this in position and brush it with cold water. Top with the pastry lid and seal the edges. Knock up and flute the edges with a knife (see page 63) and glaze the top with milk. Make a couple of slits in the centre of the pie to let out steam and bake it in the centre of the oven for 30 minutes.

Chicken and Cucumber Flan

Illustrated on page 46

Serves 6

175 g/6 oz Shortcrust Pastry (page 58)
225 g/8 oz cooked chicken
3 spring onions
¼ cucumber
300 ml/½ pint natural yogurt
pinch of dried tarragon
2 free-range eggs
freshly ground black pepper

Roll the pastry out on a lightly floured surface and use it to line a 20 cm/8 in flan dish. Bake the flan blind (see page 62) in a moderately hot oven (200 C, 400 F, gas 6) for 10 minutes.

Meanwhile, prepare the filling. Finely chop the chicken. Trim the spring onions and chop them very finely. Peel and dice the cucumber. Mix all these ingredients together and spread the mixture evenly inside the cooked pastry case. Lower the oven temperature to moderate (180 C, 350 F, gas 4). Beat the yogurt with the tarragon and eggs and season with pepper. Pour the liquid over the flan and bake it for 30 minutes, until firm to the touch. Serve cold.

Pepperoni Tartlets

Illustrated on pages 72–73

Makes 4 individual tartlets

225 g/8 oz Shortcrust Pastry (page 58)
100 g/4 oz onion
1 clove garlic
2 teaspoons oil
1 red pepper
¼ teaspoon marjoram
2 free-range eggs
150 ml/¼ pint natural yogurt
freshly ground black pepper
50 g/2 oz Cheddar cheese, grated

Roll the pastry out on a floured surface and use it to line four 10 cm/4 in tartlet tins. Bake them blind (see page 62) in a moderately hot oven (200 C, 400 F, gas 6) for 10 minutes.

Finely chop the onion and crush the garlic. Sauté these together in the oil for a few minutes without browning them. Deseed and finely chop the pepper. Beat the marjoram with the eggs and yogurt and season with pepper. Divide the onion mixture between the cooked tartlet cases and scatter the chopped red pepper on top. Pour some of the yogurt mixture into each, sprinkle with grated cheese and bake the tartlets in the centre of the oven for 20–25 minutes, until golden brown and set. Serve hot or cold.

Oaty Leek Pie

Illustrated on pages 60–61

Serves 3–4

1 quantity Oat Pastry (page 58)
450 g/1 lb leeks
2 free-range eggs
100 g/4 oz low fat soft cheese
few sprigs of fresh rosemary or ½ teaspoon dried rosemary
freshly ground black pepper
skimmed milk to glaze

Put the pastry in the refrigerator while you make the filling.

Set the oven at moderately hot (200 C, 400 F, gas 6). Wash the leeks thoroughly, trim them and cut them into 1 cm/½ in-thick rings. Steam the rings lightly or simmer them in a little water for 5 minutes, until just soft. Drain and place them in the bottom of a deep pie dish. Beat the eggs with the soft cheese, rosemary and pepper and pour the mixture over the leeks.

Roll the pastry out on a lightly floured surface to a piece 1 cm/½ in larger all round than the top of the pie dish. Cut a 1 cm/½ in-wide strip from all the way round the pastry and position this on the rim of the dish. Brush with cold water. Put the pastry lid on the pie, sealing it to the pastry rim, and knock up and flute the edges with the back of a knife (see page 63). Glaze the top of the pie with milk, make a couple of vents in it for steam to escape and bake it for 25–30 minutes, until the filling is firm when tested with a skewer. Serve hot from the oven.

OVERLEAF Pepperoni Tartlets (page 71), Picnic Pasties (page 67), Tuna Fish Plait (right of picture, page 74), Herb Roll (page 42), Rock Cakes (page 97), Apricot Slices (page 117)

Tuna Fish Plait

Illustrated on pages 72–73

Serves 4–5

225 g/8 oz Flaky or Rough Puff Pastry (page 59)
1 (198-g/7-oz) can tuna in brine
50 g/2 oz onion
50 g/2 oz button mushrooms
½ small red pepper, deseeded
½ teaspoon dried oregano
1 free-range egg, beaten
1 tablespoon vegetable stock
freshly ground black pepper
skimmed milk and 25 g/1 oz grated cheese to glaze

Leave the pastry in the refrigerator while you prepare the filling.

Set the oven at hot (220 C, 425 F, gas 7). Drain and flake the tuna and place it in a bowl. Finely chop the onion, mushrooms and red pepper and stir them into the fish with the oregano. Bind the fish mixture with the beaten egg, add the stock and sprinkle in black pepper to taste.

On a lightly floured surface, roll the pastry out to a 25 × 20 cm/10 × 8 in rectangle, about 5 mm/¼ in thick, with the shortest side nearest to you. Trim the edges and arrange the tuna filling down the centre to within 1 cm/½ in of the top and bottom of the rectangle and 5 cm/2 in of either side. Make diagonal cuts in the pastry on each side of the filling, 1 cm/½ in apart. Brush the pastry with water and bring the 1 cm/½ in-wide strips alternately over the tuna filling, overlapping down the centre to make a plait. Fold over the top and bottom pieces of pastry. Roll out any trimmings to a thin strip, twist it and arrange it down the centre of the plait. Glaze the pastry with milk, sprinkle it with grated cheese and bake it at the top of the oven for 25–30 minutes, until well risen and firm. Serve the tuna plait hot or cold.

Fish and Egg Pie

Illustrated on page 49

Serves 4

225 g/8 oz Flaky or Rough Puff Pastry (page 59)
450 g/1 lb cod or coley fillet
150 ml/¼ pint white wine or cider (optional)
sprig of fresh fennel or ¼ teaspoon dried fennel
4 black peppercorns
3 free-range eggs, hard-boiled
100 g/4 oz onion
50 g/2 oz unsalted butter or soft vegetable margarine
50 g/2 oz wholemeal flour
150 ml/¼ pint skimmed milk
freshly ground black pepper
beaten egg to glaze

Leave the pastry in the refrigerator to rest while you prepare the filling. Put the fish in a large saucepan with the wine or cider, if used, and add enough cold water to cover. Alternatively, simply use all cold water for the liquid. Add the fennel and black peppercorns. Heat the pan gently and poach the fish for about 10 minutes, until just firm. Drain, reserving 300 ml/½ pint stock.

Set the oven at hot (220 C, 425 F, gas 7). Chop the eggs. Finely chop the onion and soften it in the butter or margarine for a few minutes, without browning. Stir in the flour and cook for 1 minute. Gradually pour in the milk and reserved fish stock, beating well to make a smooth, glossy sauce. Stir in the chopped egg. Flake the fish, add it to the pan, season the mixture with pepper to taste and keep it warm while you prepare the pastry case.

Roll the pastry out on a floured surface to a piece 5 mm/¼ in thick and 1 cm/½ in larger all round than the top of a deep pie dish. Cut a 1 cm/½ in-wide strip from all round the pastry piece and position it on the rim of the dish. Pour in the filling. Brush the pastry strip with water and gently lift the pastry lid on to the filling.

Trim away any excess pastry and seal the edges. Knock up and flute the edges with the back of a knife, and roll out the pastry trimmings and cut them into five leaves (see page 63). Arrange them in the centre of the pie and make a hole in the surface for steam to escape. Glaze the pie with beaten egg and bake it in the centre of the oven for 25–30 minutes, until it is well risen and golden.

Ratatouille Puff

Illustrated on page 57

Serves 4

100 g/4 oz onion
1 clove garlic
175 g/6 oz aubergine
1 tablespoon oil
225 g/8 oz tomatoes
100 g/4 oz courgettes
½ green pepper, deseeded
2 teaspoons chopped fresh
or 1 teaspoon dried basil
a little cornflour to thicken
freshly ground black pepper
225 g/8 oz Flaky Pastry (page 59)
skimmed milk to glaze

Finely chop the onion and crush the garlic. Wipe and dice the aubergine. Heat the oil in a pan and sauté the onion, garlic and aubergine together over a low heat. Peel the tomatoes (see Pizza Pie, page 44), add them to the pan, bring the mixture to the boil and simmer it for 5 minutes. Slice the courgettes, finely chop the pepper and stir both into the pan with the basil. Simmer the vegetables for 20 minutes. Blend a little cornflour with cold water, add this to the pan and boil, stirring, for 1 minute, until the juice has thickened. Season the ratatouille with freshly ground black pepper.

Set the oven at hot (220 C, 425 F, gas 7). Roll the pastry out on a floured surface to a 25 cm/10 in square. Trim the edges. Place the filling in the centre and dampen the edges with cold water. Fold the four corners over the filling to meet in the centre, seal all the edges, glaze the puff with milk and place it on a baking tray. Bake it for 25 minutes, until the pastry is cooked and golden brown in colour. Serve hot or cold.

Prawn Puffs

Illustrated on page 57

Makes 12

50 g/2 oz soft vegetable margarine
150 ml/¼ pint cold water
65 g/2½ oz 81 or 85 per cent wheatmeal flour, sifted
2 free-range eggs
50 g/2 oz grated Cheddar or Gruyère cheese

FILLING

25 g/1 oz unsalted butter
25 g/1 oz 81 or 85 per cent wheatmeal flour
6 tablespoons skimmed milk
2 tablespoons single cream
freshly ground black pepper
100 g/4 oz shelled prawns
1 tablespoon canned or frozen and thawed sweet corn kernels

Set the oven at hot (220 C, 425 F, gas 7). Lightly grease a baking tray. Put the margarine and water in a saucepan and heat them together. When the margarine has melted, let the mixture boil and immediately pour in the sifted flour. Beat well and remove the pan from the heat. Continue beating until the mixture is smooth and glossy and leaves the side of the pan. Beat in one egg and continue beating until no traces of the egg remain. Do the same with the second egg. Beat in the cheese. Place dessertspoonfuls of the mixture on to the baking tray, spaced well apart, and bake the choux at the top of the oven for 15 minutes. Reduce the heat to moderately hot (190 C, 375 F, gas 5) and continue cooking for a further 10–15 minutes. Test to see if the puffs are ready: if the sides give when pressed lightly, they need a few minutes more. When quite firm, slit each one to let the steam escape and return them to the oven for a further 5 minutes. Leave them to cool on a wire rack.

Now prepare the filling. Melt the butter in a pan and stir in the flour. Cook for 1 minute, stirring. Gradually add the milk and cream, bring the mixture to the boil and boil it for 1 minute, stirring continuously, to make a thick, smooth and glossy sauce. Season it with pepper, stir in the prawns and sweet corn and use the sauce to fill the puffs. Serve at once as a starter.

Cheesy Leek Gougère

Illustrated on page 35

Serves 4

1 quantity Choux Pastry (page 64)
350 g / 12 oz leeks
40 g / 1½ oz soft vegetable margarine
40 g / 1½ oz wholemeal flour
300 ml / ½ pint skimmed milk
75 g / 3 oz farmhouse Cheddar cheese, grated
freshly ground black pepper

Set the oven at hot (220 C, 425 F, gas 7). Lightly grease a shallow, oval ovenproof dish. Place large spoonfuls of the pastry all around the inside edge of the dish and bake the choux at the top of the oven for 15 minutes. Lower the heat to moderately hot (190 C, 375 F, gas 5) and continue cooking for a further 15 minutes.

While the pastry is cooking, prepare the filling. Trim off the coarse green leaves at the tops of the leeks, and cut the leeks into 1 cm / ½ in rings. Wash thoroughly, plunge them into boiling water and cook them for 5–7 minutes, until just tender. Drain the leeks, reserving the cooking water. Melt the margarine in a pan and stir in the flour. Cook for 1 minute, then gradually stir in the milk, followed by 150 ml / ¼ pint of the leek stock, bring the sauce to the boil and boil it for 1 minute, stirring. Mix in the grated cheese, season with pepper and add the leeks. Keep the sauce warm until the gougère is ready, then pour the sauce into the centre and serve.

Savoury Spinach Choux

Illustrated on page 57

Makes 20

1 quantity Choux Pastry mixture (page 64) plus a pinch of cayenne
225 g / 8 oz fresh or frozen spinach
175 g / 6 oz low fat soft cheese
pinch of grated nutmeg
freshly ground black pepper

Make the choux pastry as directed on page 64, adding the cayenne with the flour. Set the oven at hot (220 C, 425 F, gas 7) and lightly grease two baking trays. Place teaspoonfuls of the mixture, spaced well apart, on the baking trays and bake them at the top of the oven for 15 minutes. Turn down the heat to moderately hot (190 C, 375 F, gas 5) and continue cooking until the choux pastry is cooked. Test by pressing the sides of the balls: if they give, they need a little longer. When quite firm to the touch, remove the choux from the oven, make a slit in each to let the steam escape and return them to the oven for a final 5 minutes. Transfer them to a wire rack and leave them to cool.

Wash and finely chop fresh spinach, put it wet in a heavy-based pan over a low heat and cook it, covered, for 5 minutes. Drain and chop it again. Place frozen spinach in a pan and defrost it. Heat it through for 1 minute. Mix the cooked spinach with the soft cheese, nutmeg and pepper and when the choux are cold, stuff them with the mixture. Serve them the same day, as choux pastry does not keep.

Apple Pie

Serves 6

225 g/8 oz Shortcrust Pastry (page 58)
675 g/1½ lb cooking apples
4 cloves (optional)
2 tablespoons clear honey
2 tablespoons cold water
skimmed milk to glaze

Preheat the oven to moderately hot (200 C, 400 F, gas 6). Chill the pastry in the refrigerator while you prepare the filling.

Peel, core and slice the apples and layer them in a 900 ml/1½ pint pie dish, alternating with the cloves, if used, the honey and water. Roll the pastry out on a floured surface to a piece 2.5 cm/1 in larger all round than the top of the pie dish. Cut a 2.5 cm/1 in-thick strip from all round the piece and place it on the rim of the dish. Brush it with cold water. Lower the pastry lid on the dish, trim away any surplus with a knife and press the edges together to seal. Knock up and flute the edges with the back of a knife (see page 63). Make a hole in the centre of the pie for steam to escape. Glaze the top with milk and bake it in the centre of the oven for 30–40 minutes.

Variations

Blackberries, plums, rhubarb, gooseberries or blackcurrants can be substituted for the apples. Omit the cloves, and add a little more honey and water to the tarter fruits.

For a fruit pie with a double crust, use half as much pastry again and line the base and sides of the dish with pastry (see page 63) before filling the pie and covering it with pastry as above. A double crust pie is best made in a shallow rather than a deep pie dish.

Orange and Raisin Cheesecake

Illustrated on page 65

Serves 4–6

100 g/4 oz Sweet Shortcrust Pastry (page 58)
2 free-range eggs, separated
2 tablespoons clear honey
225 g/8 oz low fat soft cheese
juice of 1 orange
50 g/2 oz raisins

Preheat the oven to moderately hot (200 C, 400 F, gas 6). Roll out the pastry to line an 18 cm/7 in fluted flan ring. Bake it blind (see page 62) for 10 minutes, remove the greaseproof paper and bake for a further 5 minutes. Lower the oven temperature to moderate (180 C, 350 F, gas 4).

Beat the egg yolks with the honey until thick and pale. Beat in the cheese, orange juice and raisins. Whisk the egg whites until stiff and gently fold them into the cheese mixture. Pour the filling into the flan case and bake in the centre of the oven for 25–30 minutes, until golden brown and just firm to the touch.

Baked Banana Cheesecake

Serves 4–6

100 g/4 oz Sweet Shortcrust Pastry (page 58)
2 free-range eggs, separated
2 tablespoons clear honey
225 g/8 oz low fat soft cheese
1 banana, mashed
juice of half a lemon

Preheat the oven to moderately hot (200 C, 400 F, gas 6). Roll out the pastry to line an 18 cm/7 in fluted flan ring or dish. Bake it blind (see page 62) for 10 minutes, then remove the greaseproof paper and bake for a further 5 minutes.

Lower the oven temperature to moderate (180 C, 350 F, gas 4). Beat the egg yolks with the honey until thick and pale in colour. Beat in the soft cheese, banana and lemon juice. Stiffly whisk the egg whites and gently fold them into the cheese mixture. Pour the filling into the flan case and bake for 25–30 minutes, until golden brown and just firm to the touch. Cool thoroughly.

Apple Bâteaux

Makes 8

100 g/4 oz Sweet Shortcrust Pastry (page 58)
350 g/12 oz cooking apples
2 tablespoons clear honey
juice of 1 lemon
3 red dessert apples

Preheat the oven to moderately hot (200 C, 400 F, gas 6). Use the pastry to line eight bâteau tins. Bake them blind (see page 62) for 10 minutes. Remove the greaseproof paper and bake for 5 minutes more. Gently turn out the bâteaux.

Peel, core and slice the cooking apples and cook them in a covered pan with a little water for 20–25 minutes, until reduced to a purée. Sweeten this with 1 tablespoon of the honey and divide it between the pastry cases. Core the dessert apples and cut them into fine slices. Dip these in lemon juice and arrange them upright in the pastry cases to make 'sails'. Glaze with the remaining honey and bake the bâteaux for 10 minutes. Serve hot or cold.

Franzipan

Illustrated on page 65

Serves 6

100 g/4 oz Sweet Shortcrust Pastry (page 58)
225 g/8 oz raw cane sugar marzipan
50 g/2 oz soft vegetable margarine
50 g/2 oz Muscovado sugar
1 free-range egg
25 g/1 oz ground almonds
50 g/2 oz wholemeal flour
½ teaspoon baking powder
a little skimmed milk to mix
beaten egg white to glaze

Preheat the oven to moderately hot (190 C, 375 F, gas 5). Roll the pastry out on a floured surface to fit an 18 cm/7 in fluted flan ring, allowing an extra 2.5 cm/1 in all round. Line the flan dish and keep the pastry trimmings. Knead the marzipan until pliable, roll it out to a piece to fit the flan dish and position it on top of the pastry.

Cream the margarine and sugar until light and fluffy. Beat in the egg. Sift the almonds, flour and baking powder together and add the bran left in the sieve. Gently fold the dry ingredients into the fat mixture with a metal spoon and add a little milk to give a smooth, dropping consistency.

Spread the mixture carefully over the marzipan. Roll the pastry trimmings out to fine strips, 5 mm/¼ in wide and a little over 18 cm/7 in long. Twist the strips and arrange them in a lattice pattern on top of the flan. Glaze the pastry with egg white and bake the flan in the centre of the oven for 25 minutes, until golden brown and just firm to the fingertip. Serve hot or cold. (The recipe quantities were doubled to fit a 25 cm/10 in flan ring, in the photograph on page 65.)

Honey Custard Tart

Illustrated on page 35

Serves 4

PASTRY

90 g/$3\frac{1}{2}$ oz wholemeal flour
40 g/$1\frac{1}{2}$ oz ground almonds
65 g/$2\frac{1}{2}$ oz soft vegetable margarine
grated rind of half a lemon
1 free-range egg
1 tablespoon cold water

FILLING

2 free-range eggs
2 teaspoons clear honey
300 ml/$\frac{1}{2}$ pint skimmed milk
1 teaspoon grated nutmeg

Preheat the oven to moderately hot (200 C, 400 F, gas 6). Sift the flour and almonds into a bowl and rub in the margarine until the mixture resembles fine breadcrumbs. Stir in the grated lemon rind. Make a well in the centre and break in the egg. Gradually work the egg into the flour mixture, adding a little water, if necessary, to make a soft, but not sticky, dough. Roll the dough out on a lightly floured surface to fit an 18 cm/7 in fluted flan ring or dish and bake the flan blind (see page 62) for 10 minutes.

Lower the oven temperature to moderate (160 C, 325 F, gas 3). Lightly beat the eggs with the honey. Heat the milk until warm and pour it on to the beaten eggs. Stir well and strain the mixture into the pastry case. Sprinkle the top with nutmeg and bake the tart for 30–40 minutes, until the custard has set. Serve cold.

Top to bottom: Simnel Cake (page 95), Banana and Walnut Cake (page 94), Cinnamon Apricot Cake (page 93)

Almond Slices

Illustrated on page 65

Makes 10

PASTRY

50 g/2 oz soft vegetable margarine
100 g/4 oz wholemeal flour
1 egg yolk
cold water to mix

FILLING

50 g/2 oz soft vegetable margarine
50 g/2 oz light Muscovado sugar
1 egg yolk
75 g/3 oz ground almonds
50 g/2 oz wholemeal flour
25 g/1 oz desiccated coconut
2 tablespoons skimmed milk
2 egg whites
a few split almonds to decorate

Set the oven at moderate (180 C, 350 F, gas 4). Rub the margarine into the flour until the mixture resembles fine breadcrumbs. Add the egg yolk and just enough cold water to mix to a soft, but not sticky, dough. Roll the dough out to line a 20 cm/8 in shallow square cake tin.

Now prepare the filling. Cream the margarine with the sugar until light and fluffy. Beat in the egg yolk. In a separate bowl, sift the ground almonds and flour together and add the coconut. Gently fold the dry ingredients and skimmed milk into the fat mixture with a metal spoon. Whisk the egg whites until stiff, fold them in and pile the cake mixture into the pastry case. Lightly smooth the top, sprinkle it with a few split almonds and bake the cake for 20–25 minutes, until well risen and just firm. Leave to cool in the tin and cut it into ten slices.

Sponge Fruit Flan

Illustrated on pages 60–61

Serves 4–6

2 free-range eggs
2 tablespoons clear honey
50 g/2 oz wholemeal flour

FILLING

about 450 g/1 lb fresh fruit (dessert apples, pears or gooseberries, strawberries, apricots) or canned fruit in natural juice
1 teaspoon arrowroot
150 ml/¼ pint orange or apple juice or juice from the can

Grease and flour a 20 cm/8 in sponge flan tin and line the raised base with a piece of greased greaseproof paper. Set the oven at moderately hot (200 C, 400 F, gas 6). Put the eggs and honey in a bowl and stand the bowl over a pan of hot water. Whisk them hard for several minutes until thick and creamy and the whisk, when lifted, leaves a ribbon trail in the mixture. Sift the flour, adding the bran left in the sieve, and carefully fold it into the whisked egg. Pour the mixture into the tin and bake it for 25–30 minutes. Leave the flan to cool in the tin for 2 minutes, then gently turn it out (a wet cloth placed over the base will help to ease it out). Cool on a wire rack and fill the flan when cold.

Prepare the chosen fruit as appropriate: peel, core and slice apples and pears, top and tail gooseberries, hull stawberries and so on. Arrange the fruit neatly in the flan case. Whisk the arrowroot into the fruit juice and gently bring the mixture to the boil in a pan. Boil for 1 minute, stirring, until the liquid has become clear, then pour it over the fruits in the flan to make a glaze.

To make a pastry fruit flan, see below.

Variation

To make a pastry fruit flan, roll out 100 g/4 oz Sweet Shortcrust Pastry (page 58) to fit an 18 cm/7 in fluted flan ring. Glaze the edge all the way round with beaten egg white. Bake blind (see page 62) for 10 minutes, then remove the greaseproof paper and bake it for a further 5 minutes, until the pastry is cooked through. Take the flan out of its tin and fill it when quite cold.

Apple and Mincemeat Slice

Makes 10–12 slices

175 g/6 oz Sweet Shortcrust Pastry (page 58)
6 tablespoons mincemeat
175 g/6 oz cooking apples
beaten egg white to glaze

Preheat the oven to moderately hot (200 C, 400 F, gas 6). Roll out two thirds of the pastry on a floured surface to a 25 × 20 cm/10 × 8 in rectangle. Put this in a swiss roll tin and trim the edges.

Place the mincemeat in a small bowl. Peel, core and grate the cooking apple and stir it well into the mincemeat. Spread the mixture over the pastry to within 1 cm/½ in of the edge all round. Roll out the remaining third of pastry and cut it into strips just under 1 cm/½ in wide and long enough to reach diagonally across the pastry rectangle. Arrange the strips diagonally across the mincemeat, leaving equal gaps between them. Flute the edges of the pastry all round (see page 63) and glaze with egg white. Bake in the centre of the oven for 25 minutes, until golden brown. Serve hot or cold, cut into slices.

Orange Coconut Tart

Illustrated on page 65

Serves 4

100 g/4 oz Sweet Shortcrust Pastry (page 58)
2 tablespoons no-added-sugar marmalade
50 g/2 oz soft vegetable margarine
50 g/2 oz light Muscovado sugar
1 free-range egg
25 g/1 oz desiccated coconut
50 g/2 oz wholemeal flour
½ teaspoon baking powder
juice of half an orange

Preheat the oven to moderately hot (190 C, 375 F, gas 5). Roll the pastry out on a floured surface and line an 18 cm/7 in fluted flan ring or dish. Spread the marmalade over the pastry. Cream together the margarine and sugar until light and fluffy and beat in the egg. Add the coconut and sift in the flour and baking powder, adding the bran left in the sieve. Fold the flour in with a metal spoon, followed by the orange juice, and pile the filling into the flan dish. Smooth the top lightly and bake the tart in the centre of the oven for 25–30 minutes, until the filling just springs back when touched with the fingertip. Serve hot or cold.

Eccles Cakes

Makes 16

25 g/1 oz soft vegetable margarine
1 tablespoon demerara sugar
100 g/4 oz currants
grated rind of half a lemon
½ teaspoon mixed spice
225 g/8 oz Flaky or Rough Puff Pastry (page 59)
skimmed milk to glaze

Set the oven at hot (220 C, 425 F, gas 7). Melt the margarine in a pan and stir in the sugar, currants, lemon rind and spice. Remove the pan from the heat.

Roll the pastry out on a lightly floured surface to a piece 5 mm/¼ in thick. Stamp out rounds with an 8.5 cm/3½ in fluted cutter. Place one heaped teaspoon of filling in the centre of each round and dampen the pastry edges with water. Gather up the edges over the filling and press together to seal. Turn the cakes over and place them on a baking tray, patting each one into a round. Leave them to rest for 15 minutes. Make three slits across the top of each cake, glaze them with milk and bake them at the top of the oven for 20–25 minutes. Put them on a wire rack to cool.

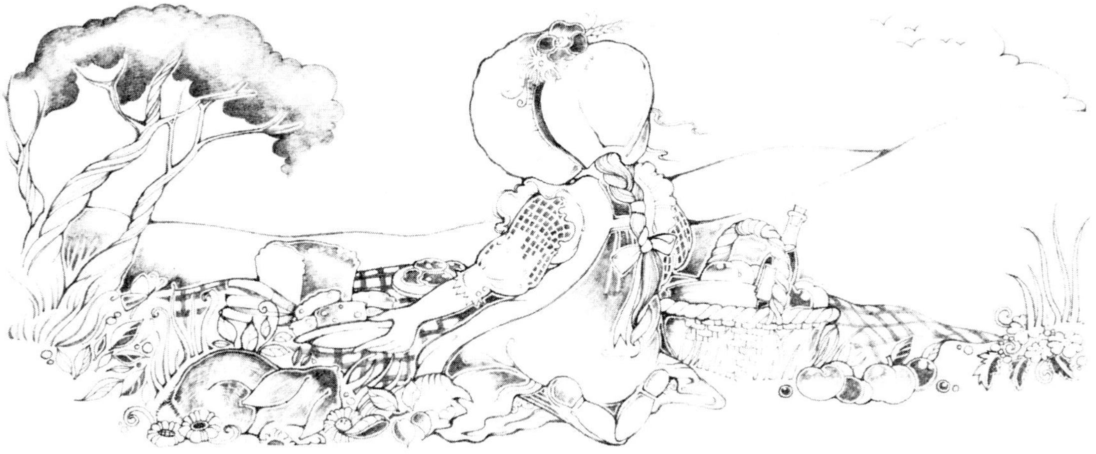

Now we come to the real tea-time treats – light sponges, creamy gâteaux, rich dark fruit loaves – there's a kind of cake to suit every occasion. Using wholefood ingredients will make any conventional recipe a good deal healthier, transforming an over-sweet, sickly cake that is high in fat to one both nutritious and satisfying and in which, moreover, subtler tastes than just sugar and butter have been allowed to develop. By exploiting the natural sweetness of dried fruits and nuts and bringing in the flavours of honey and a whole range of spices, these recipes call for far less sugar than usual. Using wholemeal flour, of course, makes the basic cake mixture much healthier than using white flour and at the same time it imparts a wonderful, nutty flavour to the finished cake. And wherever possible, the amount of fat usually called for in conventional cake recipes has been reduced.

However, this is no excuse for over-indulgence! Wholefood cakes should still be seen for what they are: treats for birthdays, visitors and special occasions, not everyday fare. Their ingredients may be healthier than many recipes – but they are still cakes!

Cake Making Terms

Creaming

This is the traditional method of making cakes, whereby the fat is blended with the sugar to give a light, fluffy texture. Creaming incorporates air, so thoroughly beating the fat and sugar together first helps to ensure a nicely risen cake. Once the fat and sugar are light and fluffy, the eggs are beaten in, one at a time. Creaming can be done with a wooden spoon, but food mixers and processors are faster. Soft vegetable margarines are best used straight from the refrigerator; harder fats need to be brought to room temperature first.

Rubbing In

For plainer cakes where the ratio of fat to flour is less than half, the fat is rubbed in. For best results, cut the fat into small pieces, drop these into the flour and rub them in with your fingertips, lifting the mixture out of the bowl and letting it drop back in as you do so. This helps to add more air to the mixture, producing a fine result. Rub in until the mixture resembles fine breadcrumbs and all the fat is evenly distributed.

Melting

The fat is melted with the sugar, honey or molasses and immediately beaten into the dry ingredients. This is the traditional way of making gingerbread and some fruit cakes.

Top to bottom: Family Fruit Cake (page 90), Carrot and Almond Cake (page 90), Honey Swiss Roll (page 91)

Whisking

Some recipes – whisked sponges and swiss rolls – do not need fat. Instead the sugar or honey and eggs are whisked together over hot water for several minutes, until thick and ropey (this can also be done in a food mixer). A good test to see if the right point has been reached is to write the letter W in the mixture by trailing a spoonful of it on the surface. If, as you make the last stroke, the first stroke is still visible, the mixture is ready. The sifted flour is then folded in and the cake is ready for baking.

A Genoese sponge is made by the same method but melted fat or oil is folded in with the flour to produce a cake that keeps slightly longer.

One-stage Cakes

This is a quick method of making sponge cakes whereby all the ingredients are beaten together thoroughly until mixed in. This method depends on using soft vegetable margarine, not hard fat, and extra raising agent is usually needed to compensate for less efficient air incorporation.

Sifting

Sifting flour before use helps to incorporate air, thus producing a lighter result. All the recipes in this chapter use wholemeal flour which, when sifted, leaves the bran in the sieve. Don't throw this away; either tip it back into the flour or use it to dust cake tins once greased. Any raising agent and spices should be sifted with the flour to ensure their even distribution.

Folding In

Many recipes tell you to 'fold' in the sifted flour, that is, to add it as gently as possible to avoid deflating the mixture. Use a metal tablespoon and slowly rotate the bowl at the same time as moving the spoon gently down the side of the bowl, under the mixture, up the other side and then over the top. Continue in this way until all the flour has been folded in. Whisked egg whites should also be added in this way.

Testing to See if a Cake is Done

To test if a sponge cake is cooked, press the top lightly with your fingertip: if it springs back, it is ready. The cake should also have shrunk a little from the sides of the tin. Fruit cakes are ready when a skewer inserted into the centre of the cake comes out clean. Another tip is to listen to the cake; if it is 'singing', it is still cooking and is not yet ready.

Cooling

Sponge cakes should be left in their tins for 2 minutes. Then gently shake the tin, banging lightly all round the sides and bottom to loosen the cake. If it still sticks in one place, try easing it with the blade of a palette knife before inverting the tin on to a wire cooling rack. A swiss roll should be turned out of its tin in the same way immediately it is taken out of the oven, so that it is still elastic enough to be rolled up. A rich fruit cake should be cooled thoroughly in its tin before being turned out on to a wire rack.

Storing

Most cakes are best when fresh, the main exception being rich fruit cakes which mature slowly and ideally should be kept for at least a week before cutting. Wrap very rich fruit cakes in greaseproof paper, then in kitchen foil, and put them in an airtight tin. Placed in a dry, dark place the cake will keep and go on improving for many months, possibly years! Other cakes, which are best eaten within a few days, should be kept in airtight containers, preferably wrapped first in foil to ensure their freshness. Cakes can also be frozen, wrapped in greaseproof paper and placed in thick polythene bags, although freezing may dry the cake out slightly after a while.

Preparing Cake Tins

It's very important to prepare cake tins properly. If you don't, the cooked cake will stick to the tin and break up when you try to turn it out, and it may be burnt round the side into the bargain.

For sponge and sandwich cakes, lightly grease the tins and place a round of greaseproof paper in the bottom. The sides of the tins should then be dusted with bran from the sieve or with a little extra wholemeal flour, and the lining paper itself greased so that it will peel off the cooked cake.

Fruit cakes need more protection, as they are baked for longer and are in greater danger of drying out round the sides.

For a round tin, place the tin upside down on a double thickness of greaseproof paper and draw round the tin. Cut along your pencil marking to make two rounds to fit the bottom of the tin. Measure round the side of the tin with a piece of string and cut out a long strip of double thickness greaseproof paper 1 cm/½ in longer than the string and 2.5 cm/1 in wider than the depth of the tin. Make a 2.5 cm/1 in crease all along the length of the strip and snip this at 1 cm/½ in intervals. Lightly grease the base and sides of the tin and put one of the greaseproof rounds inside, to line the base. Fit the long greaseproof strip inside the tin, with the slashed border sitting flat on the base, and place the second greaseproof round on top, covering the slashed edges. Grease all the lining paper.

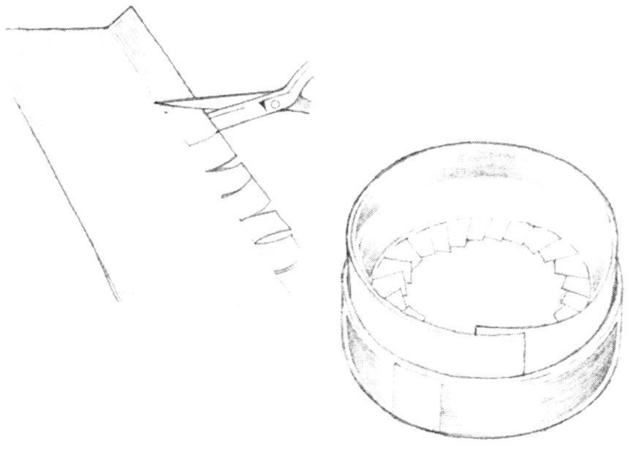

To line a square tin, place the tin upside down in the centre of a square sheet of greaseproof paper the length of whose sides are the width of the tin plus twice the depth. (A 20 cm/8 in tin with sides 5 cm/2 in deep, for instance, would need a sheet of paper measuring 30 × 30 cm/12 × 12 in.) Draw round the shape of the tin. Now cut one side of each corner of the paper from the edge to meet the outline of the tin at

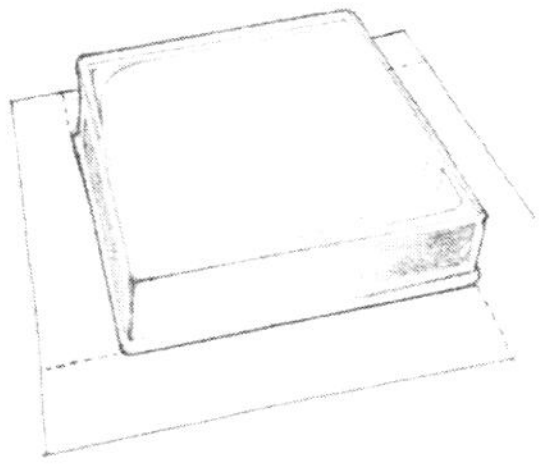

rightangles. Lightly grease the cake tin and position the paper inside with the cut corners overlapping, so that the base and sides of the tin are neatly lined. Use this method to line swiss roll tins as well. Then grease the lining paper itself so that it will peel off the cooked cake.

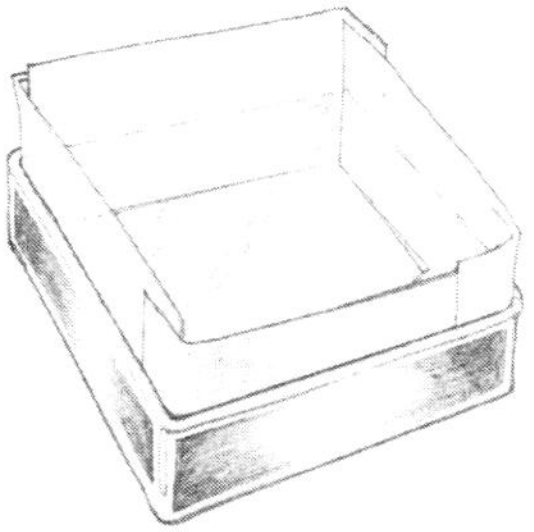

Give very rich fruit cakes which are going to be baked for several hours extra protection by tying a double thickness of brown paper or newspaper round the outside of the tin.

OVERLEAF *clockwise, from left*: Cheesy Oat Fingers (page 117), sandwiches made from Crunchy Granary Loaf (page 34), stuffed Pitta Bread (page 43), Wholemeal Bread Rolls (page 33), Carob Brownies (page 99), Sugar-free Fruit Slice (page 92), Mincemeat Flapjacks (page 116)

Family Fruit Cake

Illustrated on page 85

175 g/6 oz soft vegetable margarine
2 tablespoons honey
100 g/4 oz molasses sugar
2 free-range eggs
100 g/4 oz currants
100 g/4 oz sultanas
50 g/2 oz raisins
50 g/2 oz walnuts, finely chopped
225 g/8 oz wholemeal flour
1 teaspoon mixed spice
½ teaspoon cinnamon
2 teaspoons baking powder
a little skimmed milk to mix

Set the oven at moderate (180 C, 350 F, gas 4). Grease and line a 20 cm/8 in round cake tin. Cream together the margarine, honey and sugar until light and fluffy. Beat in the eggs, one at a time. Stir in the fruits and nuts. Sift together the flour, spices and baking powder, adding the bran left in the sieve, and fold the dry ingredients into the mixture with a metal spoon. Mix in enough milk to give a soft, dropping consistency. Turn the mixture into the tin and smooth the top. Bake the cake in the centre of the oven for 50–60 minutes, until a skewer inserted in it comes out clean. Leave the cake to cool in the tin.

Carrot and Almond Cake

Illustrated on page 85

100 g/4 oz soft vegetable margarine
75 g/3 oz Muscovado sugar
2 free-range eggs
100 g/4 oz wholemeal flour
1¼ teaspoons baking powder
40 g/1½ oz ground almonds
175 g/6 oz carrots, finely grated
25 g/1 oz flaked almonds

Grease and lightly flour a 450 g/1 lb loaf tin. Set the oven at moderate (180 C, 350 F, gas 4). Cream the margarine with the sugar until light and fluffy. Beat in the eggs, one at a time, beating well so that the mixture is thoroughly blended. Sift the flour, baking powder and ground almonds into the bowl, adding the bran left in the sieve and the grated carrot. Fold the dry ingredients gently into the mixture, using a metal spoon. Turn the mixture into the prepared loaf tin, smooth the top and sprinkle it with flaked almonds. Bake the cake in the centre of the oven for 35–40 minutes, until golden brown and just firm to the touch. Leave it to cool in the tin.

Carob Sponge

Illustrated on pages 118–119

175 g/6 oz soft vegetable margarine
100 g/4 oz Muscovado sugar
2 tablespoons clear honey
3 free-range eggs
100 g/4 oz wholemeal flour
50 g/2 oz carob powder
2 teaspoons baking powder
1 tablespoon skimmed milk
FILLING
1 banana
100 g/4 oz low fat soft cheese
dash of lemon juice
TOPPING
(optional)
1 carob bar
a few walnut halves to decorate

Set the oven at moderate (180 C, 350 F, gas 6). Grease two 18 cm/7 in sandwich tins and line the bases with greased greaseproof paper. Cream together the margarine, sugar and honey until light and fluffy. Beat in the eggs, one at a time, beating the mixture thoroughly between each addition. Sift the flour, carob powder and baking powder into a bowl. Use the bran left in the sieve to dust the greased cake tins and shake any excess back into the flour. Lightly fold the dry ingredients into the cake mixture with the milk, divide the mixture between the two tins and gently smooth the tops. Bake in the centre of the oven for 20–25 minutes, until the cakes are firm to the touch and beginning to shrink away from the sides of the tins. Leave them to cool in their tins for a few minutes, then turn them out on to a wire rack.

Mash the banana with the soft cheese and add a dash of lemon juice. When the cakes are cold, spread the filling on one sponge and place the second sponge on top. Break the carob bar, if used, into pieces and melt them in a small bowl over a pan of hot water. Pour the carob quickly over the top of the cake, smoothing it with a knife. Decorate the topping with a few walnut halves when set.

Honey Swiss Roll

Illustrated on page 85

3 free-range eggs
75 g/3 oz clear honey
75 g/3 oz wholemeal flour
3 tablespoons no-added-sugar raspberry or strawberry jam

Grease and line a swiss roll tin. Set the oven at hot (220 C, 425 F, gas 7). Place the eggs and honey in a large mixing bowl and whisk them together. If you are doing this by hand, the mixture will thicken more quickly if the bowl is stood over a pan of hot water. Whisk the mixture until it is pale and smooth and thick and the whisk, when lifted, leaves a ribbon trail on the surface. Sift the flour and use the bran remaining in the sieve to dust the lined tin. Fold the flour gently into the whisked mixture with a metal spoon. When thoroughly blended, pour the mixture into the tin and bake it in the centre of the oven for 8–10 minutes, until the sponge is beginning to shrink away from the sides of the tin and springs back when touched.

Have a sheet of greaseproof paper ready on your worktop and quickly turn out the cooked sponge on to it. If the cake doesn't at once come out of its tin, place a wet towel on top of the tin for a few seconds before trying again. Peel away the lining paper and trim the crusty edges with a knife. Spread the jam over the whole sponge and roll it up while it is still warm, using the greaseproof paper to help you. Leave the swiss roll wrapped in the paper to cool.

Coffee Honey Gâteau

Illustrated on pages 118–119

Serves 6–8

3 free-range eggs
3 tablespoons clear honey
65 g/2½ oz wholemeal flour
15 g/½ oz ground hazelnuts
2 teaspoons instant decaffeinated coffee granules dissolved in 1 tablespoon hot water
2 teaspoons sunflower oil

FILLING

300 ml/½ pint whipping cream or 225 g/8 oz low fat soft cheese
225 g/8 oz fresh fruit (strawberries, raspberries, bananas) or fruit canned in natural juice, well-drained

Grease and base-line two 18 cm/7 in sandwich tins. Set the oven at moderate (180 C, 350 F, gas 4). Put the eggs and honey in a large mixing bowl and whisk them until pale, thick and foamy and the whisk, when lifted, leaves a ribbon trail in the mixture. Sift together the flour and hazelnuts and use the bran remaining in the sieve to dust the sandwich tins. Fold the dry ingredients into the mixture together with the dissolved coffee and the oil and pour the mixture into the prepared tins. Bake the sponges in the centre of the oven for 20–25 minutes, until they spring back when touched with the fingertip. Leave them to cool in their tins for 1 minute before turning them out and leaving them to cool on wire cooling racks.

Whip the cream, if used, until stiff. Keep some whole pieces of fruit on one side and roughly chop the rest. Mix the chopped fruit into half the whipped cream or soft cheese and sandwich the cakes together with the mixture. Spread the remaining cream or cheese on top of the gâteau and decorate it with the reserved fruits.

Sugar-free Fruit Slice

Illustrated on pages 88–89

Cuts into 12 slices

350 g/12 oz cooking apples
50 g/2 oz dried apricots
50 g/2 oz blanched almonds
50 g/2 oz carrots
100 g/4 oz raisins
100 g/4 oz sultanas
225 g/8 oz wholemeal flour
2 teaspoons baking powder
¾ teaspoon ground cinnamon
¾ teaspoon mixed spice
pinch of nutmeg
100 g/4 oz soft vegetable margarine
1 free-range egg, lightly beaten
1 tablespoon skimmed milk

Peel, core and slice the apples. Put them in a saucepan with 1 tablespoon cold water and cook them gently for 20–25 minutes, until they are soft and pulpy and can be mashed to a purée. Leave to cool.

Set the oven at moderate (160 C, 325 F, gas 3). Grease and line a 20 cm/8 in square cake tin. Chop the apricots and almonds and scrub and grate the carrots. Mix these ingredients with the raisins and sultanas. Sift the flour, baking powder and spices into a mixing bowl and add the bran left in the sieve. Rub in the margarine until the mixture resembles fine breadcrumbs. Stir in the dried fruit mixture, the apple purée and the beaten egg and beat everything well together to mix thoroughly. Add the milk to give a dropping consistency. Smooth the mixture into the prepared cake tin and bake it in the centre of the oven for 45–60 minutes, until a skewer inserted in the centre comes out clean. Leave the cake to cool in the tin before cutting it into 12 slices.

Date and Walnut Granary Cake

Illustrated on pages 118–119

275 g/10 oz Granary flour
2½ teaspoons baking powder
1 teaspoon mixed spice
100 g/4 oz soft vegetable margarine
225 g/8 oz chopped dates
75 g/3 oz walnuts, finely chopped
75 g/3 oz Muscovado sugar
1 dessert apple
1 free-range egg
150 ml/¼ pint skimmed milk

Grease and line an 18 cm/7 in round cake tin. Set the oven at moderate (180 C, 350 F, gas 4). Place the flour, baking powder and spice in a mixing bowl and rub in the margarine until the mixture resembles fine breadcrumbs. Stir in the dates, walnuts and sugar. Peel, core and grate the apple and add it to the bowl. Whisk the egg lightly with the milk and beat the liquid into the cake mixture, mixing it in thoroughly. Turn the mixture into the prepared tin and bake it in the centre of the oven for 45–55 minutes, until a skewer inserted in the centre comes out clean. The cake should be just firm to the touch. Leave it to cool in the tin.

Cinnamon Apricot Cake

Illustrated on page 80

225 g/8 oz wholemeal flour
1 teaspoon cinnamon
2 teaspoons baking powder
100 g/4 oz soft vegetable margarine
50 g/2 oz light Muscovado sugar
100 g/4 oz dried apricots, chopped
1 tablespoon clear honey
1 free-range egg
1–2 tablespoons skimmed milk

Grease and line an 18 cm/7 in round cake tin. Set the oven at moderate 180 C, 350 F, gas 4). Sift the flour, cinnamon and baking powder into a bowl, adding the bran left in the sieve. Rub in the margarine until the mixture resembles fine breadcrumbs. Stir in the sugar and chopped apricots. Whisk together the honey, eggs and milk and beat the liquid thoroughly into the cake mixture. Turn the mixture into the prepared cake tin and bake it in the centre of the oven for 50–55 minutes, or until the cake is just firm to the touch and a skewer inserted in the centre comes out clean. Leave it to cool in the tin.

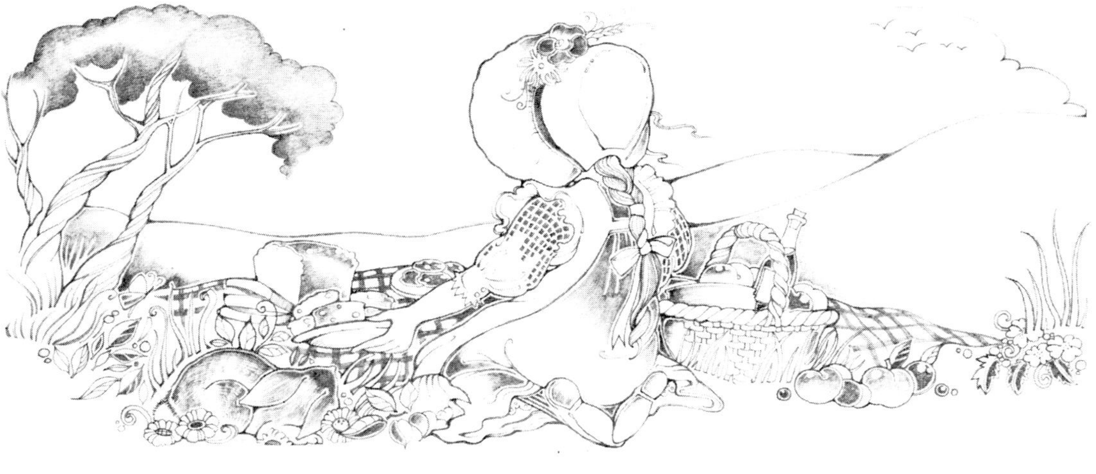

Banana and Walnut Cake

Illustrated on page 80

3 ripe bananas
2 tablespoons clear honey
6 tablespoons vegetable oil
1 free-range egg
225 g/8 oz wholemeal flour
2 teaspoons baking powder
½ teaspoon cinnamon
50 g/2 oz walnuts, finely chopped

Grease and line an 18 cm/7 in round cake tin. Set the oven at moderate (180 C, 350 F, gas 4). Put the bananas in a bowl and mash them with a fork. Add the honey and oil and beat together until well blended. Break in the egg and beat again. Sift together the flour, baking powder and cinnamon, adding the bran left in the sieve. Carefully fold the dry ingredients and the walnuts into the cake mixture, using a metal spoon. Transfer the mixture to the prepared cake tin, smooth the top and bake it in the centre of the oven for 30 minutes, until it is just firm to the touch and a skewer inserted in it comes out clean. Leave the cake to cool in the tin.

Gingerbread

Illustrated on page 96

225 g/8 oz wholemeal flour
1½ tablespoons ground ginger
½ teaspoon mixed spice
½ teaspoon bicarbonate of soda
75 g/3 oz soft vegetable margarine
75 g/3 oz Muscovado sugar
3 tablespoons molasses
2 tablespoons clear honey
1 free-range egg
150 ml/¼ pint skimmed milk

Set the oven at moderate (160 C, 325 F, gas 3). Grease and line an 18 cm/7 in square cake tin. Sift the flour, ginger, spice and bicarbonate of soda into a mixing bowl. Place the margarine, sugar, molasses and honey together in a pan and heat the mixture gently until the margarine has melted. Beat together the egg and milk and pour the liquid on to the flour, followed by the melted fat and sweeteners. Beat all the ingredients well together, pour the mixture into the prepared tin and bake it in the centre of the oven for 50–60 minutes. Leave the gingerbread to cool in its tin, then cut into squares or shapes as liked.

Simnel Cake

Illustrated on page 80

This is a rich but light cake. Though traditional for Easter, it could be made all the year round; simply omit the icing.

175 g/6 oz soft vegetable margarine
150 g/5 oz Muscovado sugar
3 free-range eggs
225 g/8 oz wholemeal flour
2½ teaspoons baking powder
50 g/2 oz ground almonds
¾ teaspoon cinnamon
100 g/4 oz raisins
100 g/4 oz sultanas
150 g/5 oz currants
50 g/2 oz split almonds, finely chopped
grated rind of a lemon
2 tablespoons skimmed milk
1 tablespoon sugar-free apricot jam
1 (227-g/8-oz) packet raw sugar marzipan
beaten egg white to glaze

Grease and line a 20 cm/8 in round cake tin. Set the oven at moderate (160 C, 325 F, gas 3). Cream together the margarine and sugar until light and fluffy. Beat in the eggs, one at a time. Sift in the flour, baking powder, the ground almonds and cinnamon and sprinkle in the bran remaining in the sieve. Add all the dried fruits, the chopped almonds and lemon rind and fold all the ingredients in with a metal spoon, adding the milk to mix. Pile the mixture into the cake tin and press it down gently, smoothing the top. Bake the cake in the centre of the oven for 1¾–2 hours, until a skewer inserted in the centre comes out clean. Leave it to cool in the tin.

When quite cold, brush the top of the cake with apricot jam. Roll out the marzipan on a surface lightly dusted with icing sugar to a round 5 cm/2 in larger in diameter than the top of the cake. Place the round on the cake, trim the surplus marzipan with a sharp knife and flute the edge (see page 63). Use the marzipan trimmings to make 11 small balls. Brush these with beaten egg white, place them on a baking tray and grill them gently until golden brown. Arrange them round the edge of the cake top.

Christmas Cake

This recipe is also suitable for celebration cakes – weddings, christenings, anniversaries and so on.

275 g/10 oz currants
225 g/8 oz sultanas
100 g/4 oz raisins
50 g/2 oz dried apricots, chopped
75 g/3 oz almonds, blanched and finely chopped
grated rind of 2 lemons
2 tablespoons sherry or brandy (optional)
200 g/7 oz wholemeal flour
1¼ teaspoons mixed spice
½ teaspoon ground nutmeg
50 g/2 oz ground almonds
1 tablespoon molasses
175 g/6 oz molasses sugar
175 g/6 oz soft vegetable margarine or unsalted butter
4 free-range eggs

Grease and line an 18 cm/7 in square or a 20 cm/8 in round cake tin. Set the oven at cool (140 C, 275 F, gas 1). Mix together all the dried fruits, the chopped almonds, grated lemon rind and the sherry or brandy, if used. Sift the flour with the spices and ground almonds. Put the molasses, the sugar and the margarine in a very large mixing bowl and cream them together until light and fluffy. Beat the eggs and gradually add them to the sugar and fat mixture, a little at a time, beating well between each addition. Pour the sifted flour and spices and the dried fruit mixture into the bowl and gradually fold these ingredients in, using a metal spoon, until everything is thoroughly mixed. Spoon the cake mixture into the tin, pressing down well, and bake it for about 3 hours. Check the cake by piercing it with a skewer. If the skewer emerges clean and the cake itself has stopped hissing, it is ready. Leave it to cool in the tin and wrap it in kitchen foil until needed.

Clockwise, from left: Orange and Walnut Buns (page 98), Gingerbread (page 94), Date and Oat Muffins (page 98)

Rock Cakes

Illustrated on pages 72–73

Makes 16

225 g/8 oz wholemeal flour
2 teaspoons baking powder
½ teaspoon cinnamon
¼ teaspoon ground nutmeg
75 g/3 oz soft vegetable margarine
25 g/1 oz demerara sugar
50 g/2 oz dried apricots, finely chopped
50 g/2 oz dates, finely chopped
50 g/2 oz sultanas
1 free-range egg to mix, beaten
2 tablespoons skimmed milk

Preheat the oven to moderately hot (200 C, 400 F, gas 6) and grease two baking trays. Sift the flour into a bowl with the baking powder and spices and add the bran left in the sieve. Rub in the margarine until the mixture resembles fine breadcrumbs. Stir in the sugar, chopped apricots, dates and sultanas and bind all the ingredients together with the beaten egg and milk, using a knife to mix to a soft dough. Place dessertspoonfuls of the dough on the prepared baking trays, spacing them well apart. Bake the rock cakes at the top of the oven for 10–15 minutes, until golden brown and firm to the touch. Leave them to cool on wire racks and eat the same day.

Date and Oat Muffins

Illustrated on page 96

Makes 8

1 dessert apple
100 g/4 oz wholemeal flour
100 g/4 oz oatmeal
2 teaspoons baking powder
½ teaspoon mixed spice
pinch of nutmeg
¼ teaspoon cinnamon
40 g/1½ oz soft vegetable margarine
75 g/3 oz dates, chopped
1 tablespoon clear honey
150 ml/¼ pint skimmed milk
1 free-range egg

Preheat the oven to moderately hot (200 C, 400 F, gas 6) and grease eight muffin pans or place paper bun cases into eight patty tins. Peel, core and grate the apple. Sift the flour into a mixing bowl and add the bran left in the sieve. Stir in the oatmeal, baking powder and spices. Rub in the margarine. Add the chopped dates and grated apple and stir everything well together. In a separate bowl, whisk together the honey, milk and egg. Pour the liquid on to the dry ingredients. Beat the mixture well, divide it between the muffin pans or bun cases and bake the muffins in the oven for 15–20 minutes, until just firm to the touch. Serve hot or cold.

Orange and Walnut Buns

Illustrated on page 96

Makes 12

100 g/4 oz soft vegetable margarine
75 g/3 oz Muscovado sugar
2 free-range eggs
175 g/6 oz wholemeal flour
3 teaspoons baking powder
75 g/3 oz walnuts, chopped
grated rind of an orange
4 tablespoons fresh orange juice

Set the oven at moderate (180 C, 350 F, gas 4). Place paper cases into 20 patty tins. Put the margarine and sugar in a mixing bowl and cream them together until light and fluffy. Beat in the eggs, one at a time, beating thoroughly between each addition. Sift the flour and baking powder into the bowl. Add the chopped nuts and the orange rind and juice and fold all the ingredients in with a metal tablespoon. Divide the mixture among the paper cases and bake the buns in the centre of the oven for 15–20 minutes, or until just firm to the touch. Transfer them to a wire rack and leave them to cool.

Apricot and Coconut Fingers

Makes 10–12

100 g/4 oz wholemeal flour
1 teaspoon baking powder
½ teaspoon cinnamon
pinch of nutmeg
pinch of ground ginger
75 g/3 oz demerara sugar
75 g/3 oz sultanas
75 g/3 oz dried apricots, chopped
50 g/2 oz desiccated coconut
2 small free-range eggs, beaten
40 g/1½ oz soft vegetable margarine, melted

Set the oven at moderate (180 C, 350 F, gas 4). Grease an 18 cm/7 in shallow, square cake tin. Sift the flour, baking powder and spices into a bowl and use the bran remaining in the sieve to dust the cake tin. Shake any surplus bran into the mixing bowl. Stir in the sugar, sultanas, apricots and coconut. Beat in the eggs and melted margarine, mix everything thoroughly and turn the mixture into the prepared tin. Smooth the top and bake the cake in the centre of the oven for 25–30 minutes, until just firm to the touch. Leave it to cool in the tin and cut it into fingers when cold.

Carob Brownies

Illustrated on pages 88–89

Makes 8

100 g/4 oz soft vegetable margarine
1 tablespoon honey
75 g/3 oz molasses sugar
2 free-range eggs
25 g/1 oz carob powder
100 g/4 oz wholemeal flour
1 teaspoon baking powder
50 g/2 oz raisins
50 g/2 oz walnuts, finely chopped
1 tablespoon skimmed milk

Set the oven at moderate (180 C, 350 F, gas 4). Lightly grease a 20 cm/8 in shallow, square cake tin. Cream the margarine with the honey and sugar until light and fluffy. Beat in the eggs, one at a time. Sift in the carob, flour and baking powder and use the bran remaining in the sieve to dust the cake tin. Add the raisins, chopped walnuts and the milk and fold all the ingredients into the mixture with a metal spoon. Spread the mixture into the prepared tin and bake it in the centre of the oven for 20–25 minutes, until just firm to the touch. Leave the cake to cool in its tin for a few minutes, then turn it out and leave it to cool on a wire rack. When cold, cut it into 8 pieces, or more if you prefer.

SCONES & BISCUITS

Scones are perhaps the ideal tea-time fare for lovers of baked goodies who are also health-conscious. Not only are they lower in fat and sugar than other cakes; they are also extremely versatile. Dried fruits, nuts and spices can all be added to the basic mixture to make sweet scones, while cheese, herbs and nuts will flavour savoury ones and Granary flour can be used instead of wholemeal to give extra bite.

The secret of making scones is to cook them at a high heat so that they rise quickly without drying out. In fact, scones all used to be baked on a griddle rather than in the oven; now only drop scones are cooked in this way. Both drop scones and oven-baked scones are best wrapped in a clean tea towel until needed and eaten the same day they are made.

Biscuits come in many different shapes, sizes and flavours. The word biscuit comes from the French and literally means 'baked twice'. The short, crisp texture of a good biscuit is achieved by various different methods of mixing. Some recipes are prepared by creaming the fat with the sugar, others by rubbing the fat into the flour and yet others by melting the fat first. Whatever the method, wholemeal flour is used every time, sifted first to make it as light as possible. Some of the recipes employ a raising agent to give the biscuit a slightly risen texture when cooked.

Shortbread is traditionally made with white flour, white sugar and butter. We have substituted wholemeal flour and a little raw cane sugar to give just a touch of sweetness, but we have kept the butter for the characteristic shortness of texture and rich flavour it gives to shortbread, both hard to achieve with margarine. Cinnamon Shorties are also made with butter for the same reason, but for recipes which contain plenty of flavouring ingredients and where such a short texture is not desirable, a margarine, preferably one made from vegetable oils, high in polyunsaturated fatty acids, will work perfectly well.

Biscuit dough may be rolled out thinly and stamped into rounds using pastry cutters, it may be baked in a slab and cut into fingers once cooked or may be dropped in spoonfuls, spaced well apart, on to a baking tray. Alternatively, the mixture may be formed into small balls with your hands and each ball flattened slightly before baking. Or you can make refrigerator cookies, as they do in America: for these the dough is formed into a long sausage, kept in the refrigerator for up to a week and 5 mm/$\frac{1}{4}$ in-thick slices are simply cut off and baked as required.

Biscuits are baked at varying temperatures, but all need the same care to ensure that they are not overbaked. Bake biscuits until they are golden brown and set but still soft to the touch.

Top: Apple Scone Round (page 106); *centre*: Apricot and Cashew Scones (page 103); *bottom*: Sultana Scones (page 103), Cheesy Walnut Scones (page 106)

Do not cook them until they are hard as they will become dry, hard and crisp as they cool. Gently lift the cooked biscuits off the tray with a palette knife and place them on a wire cooling rack. Wait until they are quite cold before storing them in an airtight tin; any warmth left will produce condensation in the tin and soften the biscuits. Biscuits which are baked in a slab, such as shortbread, are marked into portions while the slab is still hot and left to cool in the baking tin. The portions are then cut out and stored like other biscuits.

Everyone has a flapjack recipe; this chapter contains some original ideas for adding dried fruits, seeds, coconut, mincemeat and other ingredients to the basic oat, honey and margarine mixture. There is also a nutritious cheesy flapjack containing sesame and sunflower seeds, ideal for packed lunch boxes.

Apricot and Cashew Scones

Illustrated on page 101

Makes 12

225 g/8 oz wholemeal flour
2½ teaspoons baking powder
50 g/2 oz soft vegetable margarine
100 g/4 oz dried apricots, chopped
50 g/2 oz cashew nuts, chopped
6–7 tablespoons buttermilk
skimmed milk to glaze

Preheat the oven to moderately hot (200 C, 400 F, gas 6) and grease two baking trays. Sift the flour and baking powder into a bowl and add the bran left in the sieve. Rub in the margarine until the mixture resembles fine breadcrumbs. Stir in the chopped apricots and cashew nuts. Add the buttermilk and mix it in with a knife. Bring the dough together with your fingers, turn it out on to a lightly floured surface and knead it lightly to bind it. Roll or pat the dough out until it is 1 cm/½ in thick and stamp out rounds with a pastry cutter. Arrange the rounds on baking trays and glaze them with milk. Bake the scones for 15 to 20 minutes, until firm and golden brown. Leave to cool on a wire rack, covered with a clean tea towel to prevent their drying out.

Sultana Scones

Illustrated on page 101

Makes 12

225 g/8 oz wholemeal flour
2½ teaspoons baking powder
generous pinch of nutmeg
¼ teaspoon cinnamon
50 g/2 oz soft vegetable margarine
50 g/2 oz sultanas
150 ml/¼ pint skimmed milk

Lightly grease two baking trays. Set the oven at moderately hot (200 C, 400 F, gas 6). Sift the flour, baking powder and spices into a mixing bowl and add the bran left in the sieve. Rub in the margarine until the mixture resembles fine breadcrumbs. Stir in the sultanas. Stir in all but 2 tablespoons of the milk and, using the blade of a knife, bring everything together to form a dough. Knead lightly, then roll the dough out on a floured surface until it is 1 cm/½ in thick. Stamp out 12 rounds, using a 3.5 cm/1½ in pastry cutter, and transfer these to the baking trays. Glaze the scones with the remaining milk and bake them in the centre of the oven for 10–15 minutes. Transfer them to a wire rack and leave them to cool, covered with a clean cloth (this helps to keep the scones soft).

OVERLEAF *clockwise, from top left*: Crunchy Peanut Plait (page 41), Cheese and Garlic Crown (page 41), Digestive Biscuits (page 110), Savoury Nutmeat Rolls (page 67), Curried Cheese Biscuits (page 113), Oatcakes (page 111), Savoury Seed Snaps (page 111)

Apple Scone Round

Illustrated on page 101

225 g/8 oz wholemeal flour
2 teaspoons baking powder
pinch of nutmeg
¼ teaspoon cinnamon
50 g/2 oz soft vegetable mrgarin
40 g/1½ oz Muscovado sugar
225 g/8 oz cooking apple
a little skimmed milk to mix and glaze

Preheat the oven to moderately hot (200 C, 400 F, gas 6). Sift the flour, baking powder and spices into a bowl and add the bran left in the sieve. Rub in the margarine until the mixture resembles fine breadcrumbs. Stir in the sugar. Peel, core and grate the cooking apple and mix it well into the flour mixture. Add just enough milk to bind the ingredients to a soft dough and shape the dough on a lightly floured surface into a 20 cm/8 in round. Transfer the round to a lightly greased baking tray, glaze it with milk and bake it in the centre of the oven for 20–25 minutes. Leave the scone to cool on a wire rack before serving it cut into wedges and buttered in the centre.

Cheesy Walnut Scones

Illustrated on page 101

Makes 16 small scones

225 g/8 oz wholemeal flour
2½ teaspoons baking powder
1½ teaspoons finely chopped fresh sage or ½ teaspoon dried sage
pinch of sea salt
65 g/2½ oz soft vegetable margarine
75 g/3 oz Cheddar cheese, finely grated
25 g/1 oz walnuts, finely chopped
150 ml/¼ pint skimmed milk
a little extra skimmed milk to glaze

Set the oven at hot (220 C, 425 F, gas 7). Sift the flour and baking powder into a bowl and sprinkle in the bran left in the sieve. Add the sage and salt and rub in the margarine until the mixture resembles fine breadcrumbs. Stir in 50 g/2 oz of the cheese and all the chopped walnuts, followed by the milk. Mix everything to a soft dough with a knife, bring the dough together with your hands and knead it lightly on a floured surface. Roll or press it out until 1 cm/½ in thick and, using a small pastry cutter, stamp out 16 rounds. Glaze the rounds with milk, sprinkle them with the remaining cheese and place them on a lightly greased baking tray. Bake the scones for 15–20 minutes, until well risen and golden. Transfer them to a wire cooling rack and cover them with a clean cloth.

Cheese and Granary Scones

Makes 12

225 g/8 oz Granary flour
2½ teaspoons baking powder
½ teaspoon mustard powder
¼ teaspoon cayenne
50 g/2 oz soft vegetable margarine
100 g/4 oz farmhouse Cheddar cheese, finely grated
1 free-range egg
2–3 tablespoons skimmed milk
a little skimmed milk to glaze
1 tablespoon sesame seeds

Preheat the oven to moderately hot (200 C, 400 F, gas 6). Put the Granary flour, baking powder, mustard and cayenne in a bowl and mix well together. Rub in the margarine. Stir in all but 15 g/½ oz of the cheese and add the egg. Draw the mixture together with a knife, adding enough milk to bind it to a soft dough. Transfer the dough to a lightly floured surface and roll it out to a good 1 cm/½ in thick. Stamp out 12 rounds, using a 3.5 cm/1½ in pastry cutter, and place these on lightly greased baking trays. Glaze them with milk, sprinkle them with sesame seeds and the remaining cheese and bake them in the centre of the oven for 15–20 minutes. The scones are ready when they sound hollow when tapped underneath. Leave them to cool on a wire rack, covered with a clean cloth.

Drop Scones

Illustrated on pages 118–119

Makes 25–30

225 g/8 oz wholemeal flour
3 teaspoons baking powder
25 g/1 oz Muscovado sugar
50 g/2 oz currants (optional)
2 free-range eggs
300 ml/½ pint skimmed milk

Sift the flour and baking powder into a mixing bowl and add the bran left in the sieve. Add the sugar and the currants, if used. Make a well in the centre and break in the eggs. Gradually stir in the milk, bringing the flour from round the side of the bowl into the mixture in the centre as you do so. Beat until everything is thoroughly mixed and you have a thick batter.

Lightly grease a griddle or a heavy-based frying pan and heat it until quite hot. Carefully drop the batter into the pan in tablespoonfuls, allowing each to spread before you add the next. Let the scones cook for a few minutes until bubbles rise to the surface and burst, then gently flip them over and cook them on the other side for about 3 minutes. Transfer the drop scones to a wire rack and wrap them in a clean tea towel to keep the moisture in. Eat them as soon as possible, buttered.

Cheesy Drop Scones

Illustrated on pages 118–119

Makes 20

200 g/7 oz wholemeal flour
2½ teaspoons baking powder
50 g/2 oz farmhouse Cheddar cheese, finely grated
1 tablespoon grated onion
1 free-range egg
about 250 ml/8 fl oz skimmed milk
freshly ground black pepper

Sift the flour and baking powder into a mixing bowl and add the bran remaining in the sieve. Stir in the cheese and onion. Make a well in the centre and add the egg. Gradually stir in the milk and beat the mixture to form a thick batter. Season it lightly with pepper.

Lightly grease a griddle or a heavy-based frying pan and heat it until quite hot. Drop tablespoonfuls of the batter, spaced well apart, on the griddle and cook them for a few minutes until bubbles rise to the surface and burst. Flip the scones over and cook them on the other side for 3 minutes. Leave them to cool on a wire rack, covered in a clean tea towel, and serve them buttered.

Easter Biscuits

Illustrated on page 112

Makes 24

75 g/3 oz unsalted butter or soft vegetable margarine
50 g/2 oz Muscovado sugar
1 free-range egg, separated
175 g/6 oz wholemeal flour
1 teaspoon baking powder
pinch of nutmeg
75 g/3 oz currants
grated rind of half a lemon
3 tablespoons skimmed milk to mix

Preheat the oven to moderately hot (190 C, 375 F, gas 5) and grease two baking trays. Cream the butter or margarine with the sugar until light and fluffy. Beat in the egg yolk. Sift in the flour, baking powder and nutmeg and add the currants and lemon rind. Fold all these ingredients into the mixture with a metal spoon, adding the milk to bind them. Bring the mixture together with your hands to form a soft but not sticky dough.

Transfer the dough to a lightly floured surface and roll it out 3 mm/⅛ in thick. Stamp out 24 rounds, using a 3.5 cm/1½ in pastry cutter, place these on the prepared baking trays and glaze them with the egg white. Bake the biscuits in the centre of the oven for 10–15 minutes, until golden brown. Transfer them at once to wire racks and leave them to cool and crisp up.

Clockwise, from left: Orange Shortbread (page 114), Shortbread (page 113), Cinnamon Shorties (page 114)

Christmas Biscuits

Illustrated on page 112

Makes 36

50 g/2 oz unsalted butter
50 g/2 oz soft vegetable margarine
50 g/2 oz Muscovado sugar
175 g/6 oz wholemeal flour
¼ teaspoon cinnamon
pinch of nutmeg
a little skimmed milk to bind (optional)

Preheat the oven to moderately hot (190 C, 375 F, gas 5). Cream together the butter, margarine and sugar until light and fluffy. Sift in the flour and spices, adding the bran remaining in the sieve. Using your hands, draw everything together to make a soft dough that can be rolled out; add a little milk to bind if the mixture is too dry. Roll the dough out on a lightly floured surface until 3 mm/⅛ in thick and stamp out different shapes, using small fancy biscuit cutters. Place these on baking trays and bake them at the top of the oven for 10–15 minutes, until they turn a deep brown. Transfer the biscuits to wire racks to cool and crisp up.

Almond Hearts

Illustrated on pages 118–119

Makes 20

50 g/2 oz unsalted butter or soft vegetable margarine
50 g/2 oz Muscovado sugar
1 free-range egg
150 g/5 oz wholemeal flour
40 g/1½ oz ground almonds
1 teaspoon grated lemon rind
20 whole blanched almonds

Set the oven at moderate (180 C, 350 F, gas 4). Cream the butter or margarine with the sugar until light and fluffy. Beat in the egg. Sift in the flour and ground almonds, adding the bran left in the sieve. Add the lemon rind. Fold the dry ingredients in with a metal spoon and knead the mixture lightly to produce a smooth, soft dough.

Roll the dough out on a lightly floured surface until 5 mm/¼ in thick and stamp out biscuits with a heart-shaped cutter. Press a whole almond into each to decorate. Arrange the biscuits on greased baking trays and bake them at the top of the oven for 15–20 minutes, until golden brown. Lift on to wire racks and leave them to cool.

Digestive Biscuits

Illustrated on pages 104–105

Makes 14

90 g/3½ oz wholemeal flour
40 g/1½ oz fine oatmeal
½ teaspoon baking powder
pinch of sea salt
50 g/2 oz soft vegetable margarine
1 tablespoon Muscovado sugar
2–3 tablespoons skimmed milk to mix

Set the oven at moderate (180 C, 350 F, gas 4). Lightly greast two baking trays. Sift the flour, oatmeal, baking powder and salt into a mixing bowl and add the bran left in the sieve. Rub in the margarine until the mixture resembles fine breadcrumbs. Stir in the sugar and mix in the milk with the blade of a knife. Bring the dough together and knead it lightly.

Roll the dough out on a lightly floured surface to 3 mm/⅛ in thick. Stamp out 14 rounds, using a 7.5 cm/3 in biscuit cutter. Place the rounds on the baking trays and lightly prick them with a fork. Bake the biscuits in the centre of the oven for 15 minutes, until just beginning to turn golden brown at the edges. Transfer them to wire racks to cool.

Gingerbread Men

Illustrated on page 115

Makes 5

100 g/4 oz wholemeal flour
¾ teaspoon ground ginger
½ teaspoon cinnamon
¼ teaspoon ground cloves
¼ teaspoon nutmeg
25 g/1 oz soft vegetable margarine
2 tablespoons molasses
1 tablespoon skimmed milk (optional)
currants, chopped almonds, thinly pared strips of lemon or orange rind to decorate

Set the oven at moderate (180 C, 350 F, gas 4). Lightly grease a baking tray. Sift the flour and spices into a mixing bowl. Melt the margarine in a pan with the molasses and bring the mixture to the boil. Pour it at once on to the dry ingredients and beat in thoroughly, adding the milk, if necessary, to make a soft, pliable dough.

Knead the dough lightly and turn it out on to a lightly floured surface. Roll it out to 3 mm/⅛ in thick and cut out five gingerbread men, using a cutter. Place the men on the prepared baking trays and decorate them before you bake them, using currants for eyes and buttons, almonds for noses and so on. Bake them in the centre of the preheated oven for 10–15 minutes, until dark. Leave them to cool on a wire rack before eating.

Oatcakes

Illustrated on pages 104–105

Makes 20

200 g/7 oz medium oatmeal
75 g/3 oz wholemeal flour
1 teaspoon baking powder
50 g/2 oz soft vegetable margarine
a little cold water to mix

Preheat the oven to moderately hot (190 C, 375 F, gas 5) and grease two baking trays. Mix the oatmeal, flour and baking powder in a bowl together and rub in the margarine. Add just enough cold water to bind the mixture to a soft dough and knead it lightly. Roll the dough out to a 31 × 13 cm/12½ × 5 in rectangle and mark this into ten 6 cm/2½ in squares, using a knife and ruler. Cut each square into two triangles. Carefully lift the triangles on to the baking trays and bake them in the centre of the oven for 10–15 minutes. Transfer the oatcakes to wire racks and leave them to cool.

Savoury Seed Snaps

Illustrated on pages 104–105

Makes 24

225 g/8 oz wholemeal flour
50 g/2 oz soft vegetable margarine
3 teaspoons sesame seeds
3 teaspoons poppy seeds
½ teaspoon cayenne
pinch of mustard powder
1 free-range egg
a little skimmed milk to mix and glaze

Preheat the oven to moderately hot (190 C, 375 F, gas 5) and grease two baking trays. Sift the flour into a mixing bowl and add the bran remaining in the sieve. Rub in the margarine and stir in the sesame and poppy seeds, the cayenne and mustard. Mix everything thoroughly. Add the egg and just enough milk to bind the mixture to a soft but not sticky dough. Roll the dough out on a lightly floured surface and stamp out 24 rounds, using a 5 cm/2 in plain cutter. Place the rounds on the baking trays, glaze them with milk and bake them for 15–20 minutes. Transfer the snaps to wire racks and leave them to cool.

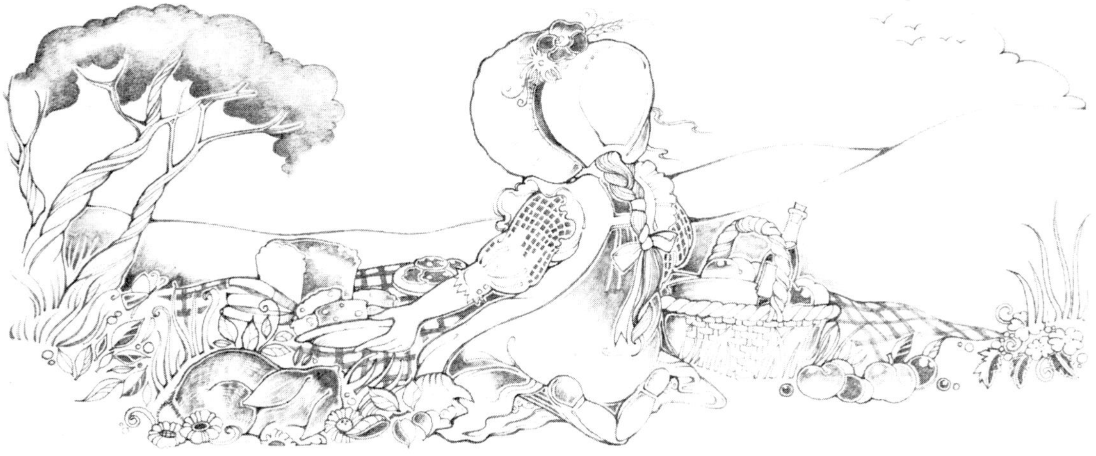

Curried Cheese Biscuits

Illustrated on pages 104–105

Makes 20

100 g/4 oz wholemeal flour
½ teaspoon ground cumin
½ teaspoon ground coriander
pinch of cayenne
pinch of turmeric
¼ teaspoon mustard powder
40 g/1½ oz soft vegetable margarine
50 g/2 oz strong Cheddar cheese, grated
1 egg yolk
about 2 tablespoons skimmed milk
beaten egg white to glaze

Set the oven at hot (220 C, 425 F, gas 7). Sift the flour into a mixing bowl and add the bran left in the sieve. Stir in the spices and mustard. Rub in the margarine until the mixture resembles fine breadcrumbs. Add the grated cheese and stir in well. Add the egg yolk and milk and mix all the ingredients with a knife to form a dough, adding a little extra milk, if required. The dough should be moist, but not sticky.

Turn the dough out on to a lightly floured surface and roll it out to 5 mm/¼ in thick. Stamp out 20 rounds, using a 5 cm/2 in biscuit cutter. Arrange the rounds on lightly greased baking trays and glaze them with egg white. Bake them in the centre of the oven for 10–15 minutes, until golden brown, then transfer the biscuits to wire racks to cool and crisp up.

Top to bottom: Coconut Kisses (page 120), Easter Biscuits (page 109), Melting Moments (page 121), Christmas Biscuits (page 109)

Shortbread

Illustrated on page 108

Cuts into 12 pieces

100 g/4 oz wholemeal flour
75 g/3 oz unsalted butter
2 teaspoons Muscovado sugar

Set the oven at moderate (180 C, 350 F, gas 4). Lightly butter an 18 cm/17 in shallow square tin. Sift the flour into a mixing bowl and add the bran left in the sieve. Rub in the butter until the mixture resembles fine breadcrumbs. Stir in the sugar. Using your hands, bring the mixture together to form a soft dough and knead it lightly until smooth and silky. Gently pat the dough out to fit inside the prepared tin and smooth the top. Prick the top several times with a fork. Lightly mark the shortbread into 12 fingers and bake it in the centre of the oven for 20–25 minutes. Retrace the portion markings and leave the shortbread to cool in the tin.

Orange Shortbread

Illustrated on page 108

Cuts into 8 pieces

150 g/5 oz wholemeal flour
75 g/3 oz unsalted butter
grated rind of an orange
1 tablespoon Muscovado sugar

Set the oven at moderate (180 C, 350 F, gas 4). Lightly butter an 18 cm/7 in sandwich tin. Sift the flour into a bowl and add the bran remaining in the sieve. Rub in the butter until the mixture resembles fine breadcrumbs. Stir in the grated rind and sugar. Bring the dough together, using your hands, and knead lightly. Press it evenly into the prepared tin. Flute the edge with your fingertips and prick the surface all over with a fork. Mark the shortbread into eight portions and bake it in the centre of the oven for 20–25 minutes, until golden brown. Retrace the markings and leave the shortbread to cool in its tin before cutting it into wedges.

Cinnamon Shorties

Illustrated on page 108

Makes 14

175 g/6 oz wholemeal flour
2 teaspoons cinnamon
100 g/4 oz unsalted butter or soft vegetable margarine
40 g/1½ oz Muscovado sugar
beaten egg white to glaze
25 g/1 oz flaked almonds

Set the oven at moderate (180 C, 350 F, gas 4). Lightly grease an 18 cm/17 in shallow square tin. Sift the flour and cinnamon into a mixing bowl and add the bran left in the sieve. Rub in the butter or margarine until the mixture resembles fine breadcrumbs. Stir in the sugar and work the mixture together to form a dough. Knead it lightly until it binds together. Press the dough evenly into the prepared tin, glaze it with egg white and sprinkle flaked almonds on top, pressing them gently on to the surface. Bake the dough in the centre of the oven for 20–25 minutes, until golden brown. Mark it into 14 fingers and leave them to cool in the tin.

Top to bottom: Gingerbread Men (page 110), Sesame and Coconut Crunch (page 116), Honey Cookies (page 120), Walnut Refrigerator Cookies (page 122)

Date Flapjacks

Makes 10

150 g/5 oz soft vegetable margarine
4 tablespoons clear honey
25 g/1 oz Muscovado sugar
100 g/4 oz chopped dates
200 g/7 oz rolled oats

Set the oven at moderate (180 C, 350 F, gas 4). Place the margarine, honey and sugar in a saucepan together and dissolve them over a low heat. Stir in the dates and oats. Smooth the mixture into a lightly greased 20 cm/8 in square baking tin and bake it for 20–25 minutes, until golden brown. Mark the cooked mixture neatly into 10 bars and leave them to cool in the tin.

Mincemeat Flapjacks

Illustrated on pages 88–89

Makes 8

75 g/3 oz soft vegetable margarine
1 tablespoon clear honey
3 tablespoons mincemeat
175 g/6 oz rolled oats

Set the oven at moderate (180 C, 350 F, gas 4). Lightly grease an 18 cm/7 in sandwich tin. Place the margarine, honey and mincemeat in a saucepan and heat them gently until the margarine has melted. Stir in the oats. Spread the mixture in the prepared tin and press it down firmly. Bake it in the centre of the oven for 20–25 minutes, until golden brown. Mark it into eight segments and leave them in the tin to cool.

Sesame and Coconut Crunch

Illustrated on page 115

Makes 15

75 g/3 oz sesame seeds
175 g/6 oz soft vegetable margarine
3 tablespoons clear honey
75 g/3 oz demerara sugar
75 g/3 oz desiccated coconut
3 tablespoons sunflower seeds
175 g/6 oz rolled oats

Spread the sesame seeds in the bottom of a grill pan and place them under a hot grill to toast lightly for a few minutes; the seeds should turn golden but not brown.

Set the oven at moderate (160 C, 325 F, gas 3). Grease a swiss roll tin. Place the margarine with the honey and sugar in a large saucepan and heat gently to melt the margarine. Stir in all the remaining ingredients, including the sesame seeds, mixing them in thoroughly. Transfer the mixture to the prepared tin and press it down well. Bake it in the centre of the oven for 25–30 minutes, until golden brown. Mark the cooked mixture into 15 squares and leave them in the tin to cool.

Cheesy Oat Fingers

Illustrated on pages 88–89

Makes 10

Ideal for lunch boxes and picnics.

150 g/5 oz rolled oats
25 g/1 oz sunflower seeds
25 g/1 oz sesame seeds
generous pinch of cayenne
¼ teaspoon mustard powder
100 g/4 oz farmhouse Cheddar cheese, finely grated
1 free-range egg
2 tablespoons skimmed milk
75 g/3 oz soft vegetable margarine, melted

Lightly grease a 20 cm/7 in square, shallow cake tin. Set the oven at moderate (180 C, 350 F, gas 4). Combine the oats, seeds, cayenne, mustard and grated cheese in a mixing bowl. Beat the egg with the milk and the melted margarine and then beat the liquid into the dry ingredients. Stir everything well together. Smooth the mixture into the tin, pressing it down firmly with the back of a fork. Bake it in the centre of the oven for 30 minutes, until golden brown. Mark the cooked mixture into 10 portions while still hot and leave them in the tin to cool.

Date Slices

Makes 16

350 g/12 oz chopped dates
4 tablespoons water
grated rind of half an orange
2 tablespoons fresh orange juice
225 g/8 oz wholemeal flour
100 g/4 oz rolled oats
75 g/3 oz demerara sugar
150 g/5 oz soft vegetable margarine

Put the dates in a pan with the water, orange rind and juice. Simmer the mixture for 5 minutes, until soft and pulpy.

Lightly grease a swiss roll tin. Set the oven at moderately hot (190 C, 375 F, gas 5). Mix together the flour, oats and sugar. Melt the margarine over a low heat and stir in the dry ingredients, combining everything thoroughly. Spread half the oat mixture in the bottom of the prepared tin and cover it with the date mixture. Spread the remaining oat mixture on top and bake in the centre of the oven for 25–30 minutes, until golden brown. Mark into 16 bars and allow them to cool in the tin.

Variation

Illustrated on pages 72–73

Substitute dried apricots for the dates.

OVERLEAF *clockwise, from top left*: Date and Walnut Granary Cake (page 93), Coffee Honey Gâteau (page 92), Drop Scones and Cheesy Drop Scones (page 107), Teacakes (page 48), Carob Orange Pinwheels (page 121), Almond Hearts (page 110), Carob Sponge (page 91)

Coconut Kisses

Illustrated on page 112

Makes 20

150 g/5 oz soft vegetable margarine
2 tablespoons clear honey
75 g/3 oz demerara sugar
100 g/4 oz rolled oats
50 g/2 oz desiccated coconut
75 g/3 oz wholemeal flour
2 teaspoons baking powder

Lightly grease two baking trays. Set the oven at moderate (180 C, 350 F, gas 4). Place the margarine, honey and sugar in a large saucepan and dissolve them over a low heat. Meanwhile, mix together the oats, coconut, flour and baking powder. When the margarine has melted completely, stir in the dry ingredients and mix thoroughly. Remove the pan from the heat. Take teaspoonsful of the mixture and roll them into balls with your hands. Flatten these slightly and put them on the baking trays, spaced well apart. Bake them in the centre of the oven for 15–20 minutes, until golden brown. Carefully lift the coconut kisses on to cooling racks where they will crisp up as they cool.

Honey Cookies

Illustrated on page 115

Makes 30

100 g/4 oz soft vegetable margarine
6 tablespoons clear honey
1 free-range egg
75 g/3 oz blanched, chopped almonds
grated rind of half an orange
50 g/2 oz sunflower seeds, toasted under a hot grill for a few minutes
1 tablespoon desiccated coconut
175 g/6 oz wholemeal flour
1 teaspoon baking powder

Preheat the oven to moderately hot (190 C, 375 F, gas 5). Grease two baking trays. Cream the margarine with the honey until light and fluffy. Beat in the egg and add the chopped almonds, orange rind, sunflower seeds and coconut. Sift in the flour and baking powder and fold them in with a metal spoon. Place teaspoonfuls of the mixture, spaced well apart, on the baking trays. Bake the biscuits at the top of the oven for 15–20 minutes, until golden brown, then transfer them to wire racks and leave them to cool.

Melting Moments

Illustrated on page 112

Makes 15

100 g/4 oz soft vegetable margarine
75 g/3 oz Muscovado sugar
1 free-range egg
50 g/2 oz chopped walnuts
1 teaspoon decaffeinated coffee granules mixed with 2 teaspoons boiling water
100 g/4 oz wholemeal flour
25 g/1 oz fine oatmeal
1 teaspoon baking powder
rolled oats to finish

Preheat the oven to moderately hot (190 C, 375 F, gas 5). Grease two baking trays. Cream together the margarine and sugar until fluffy and beat in the egg. Stir in the walnuts, coffee mixture, flour, oatmeal and baking powder. Mix everything thoroughly to form a soft dough. Roll dessertspoonfuls of the dough between your hands and toss them in the rolled oats. Flatten each slightly and place the biscuits, spaced well apart, on the baking trays. Bake them in the top of the oven for 15–20 minutes, until golden brown. Transfer them to a wire rack to cool and crisp up.

Carob Orange Pinwheels

Illustrated on pages 118–119

Makes 18

75 g/3 oz soft vegetable margarine
50 g/2 oz light Muscovado sugar
100 g/4 oz wholemeal flour
50 g/2 oz ground hazelnuts
grated rind of half an orange
1 tablespoon fresh orange juice
1 tablespoon carob powder
½ teaspoon decaffeinated coffee granules mixed with 1 tablespoon hot water
skimmed milk to glaze

Lightly grease two baking trays. Cream half the margarine with half the sugar. Sift in half the flour and all the ground hazelnuts and beat the mixture, adding the orange rind and juice, until it forms a soft dough. Chill the dough in the refrigerator for 30 minutes.

Repeat this process with the remaining fat, sugar and flour, sifting the carob powder in with the flour and adding the dissolved coffee to bind the mixture to a soft dough. Chill this dough too for 30 minutes.

Set the oven at moderate (180 C, 350 F, gas 4). Roll out both pieces of dough to 28 × 18 cm/11 × 7 in rectangles. Glaze one with milk and carefully place the second rectangle on top. Roll them up gently from the long edge, cut the roll into 18 slices and arrange these on the baking trays. Bake the pinwheels for 15–20 minutes, remove them from the oven and leave to cool on wire racks.

Walnut Refrigerator Cookies

Illustrated on page 115

Makes 28

100 g/4 oz soft vegetable margarine
100 g/4 oz Muscovado sugar
1 free-range egg
225 g/8 oz wholemeal flour
1½ teaspoons baking powder
100 g/4 oz finely chopped walnuts
1 tablespoon skimmed milk (optional)

Cream the margarine with the sugar until light and fluffy. Beat in the egg. Sift the flour and baking powder into the mixture and sprinkle in the bran remaining in the sieve. Add the walnuts and fold the dry ingredients into the mixture with a metal spoon, adding the milk, if necessary, to form a soft dough. Knead the dough lightly, divide it in two and roll each portion out to a sausage, 5 cm/2 in. in diameter. Wrap the rolls in cooking foil and place them in the refrigerator until required.

Preheat the oven to moderately hot (190 C, 375 F, gas 5). Cut 5 mm/¼ in-thick slices off the rolls; pat these out gently. Arrange the biscuits on greased baking trays and bake them at the top of the preheated oven for 15 minutes. Leave them to cool on wire racks.

Variation

Replace the walnuts with 100 g/4 oz raisins or 50 g/2 oz desiccated coconut.

INDEX